THE STRUCTURE OF WOMEN'S
NONPROFIT ORGANIZATIONS

Indiana University Center on Philanthropy Series in Governance
James R. Wood and Dwight F. Burlingame, editors

THE STRUCTURE OF WOMEN'S NONPROFIT ORGANIZATIONS

REBECCA L. BORDT

INDIANA UNIVERSITY PRESS
Bloomington and Indianapolis

The paper used in this publication meets the minimum requirements of
American National Standard for Information Sciences--Permanence of Paper for
Printed Library Materials, ANSI Z39.48-1984.

Manufactured in the United States of America

Library of Congress Cataloging-in-Publication Data

Bordt, Rebecca L., date
    The structure of women's nonprofit organizations / Rebecca L. Bordt.
    ☐☐ p. ☐☐ cm. — (IU Center on Philanthropy series in governance)
    Includes bibliographical references (p. ☐)
    ISBN 0-253-33347-4 (cl : alk. paper)
    1. Nonprofit organizations—New York (State)—New York—
Management—Case studies. 2. Women executives—New York (State)—
New York—Case studies. 3. Organization—New York (State)—New
York—Case studies. ☐ I. Title. ☐ II. Series.
    HD62.6.B67 1997
    658 .048—dc21   97-5225
    1 2 3 4 5   02 01 00 99 98 97

For Claudia, Diane and Marlene

CONTENTS

ACKNOWLEDGMENTS

Many people have contributed to this book during its various stages. Foremost, I would like to thank all the women who participated in the research by completing my questionnaire or agreeing to be interviewed. The reception I received was remarkable, given that most of the women working in nonprofit organizations are overworked and their organizations are often understaffed and financially precarious. I was struck by the women's overall energy, conviction, good humor and meticulous subway directions.

This project began as my dissertation in the department of sociology at Yale University. I am grateful for the guidance I received from my dissertation advisor, Charles Perrow, during that period and since. He encouraged me to pursue my (at the time) fledgling research idea during a conversation we had while driving from Hillsdale to New Haven. And many years later he convinced me in an e-mail message to complete my dissertation by sharing his own experience struggling to finish a book. In between, he has given me invaluable advice on the conceptualization, execution, and writing of this project.

I also want to thank the two readers on my dissertation committee: Paul DiMaggio, now at Princeton University, and Kathleen Daly,

The Structure of Women's Nonprofit Organizations

currently at Griffith University in Queensland. I took two seminars on organizational theory from Paul in 1985 and 1986. His seminars got me excited about pursuing research on women's organizations. One of Paul's many talents is his ability to find the lone kernel of insight in a pile of pedestrian ideas. He identified one such kernel hidden in a seminar memo; it is now a book. I appreciate his initial encouragement and his subsequent written comments on my dissertation. I met Kathy at the Law & Society meetings in San Diego in 1985. When we finished our brief poolside conversation, I knew immediately that I wanted to work with her when I got to Yale. I did—first as seminar member, then as research assistant, as teaching assistant, as collaborator, and friend. To this day I have kept a "KD" file of everything she has published. I feel privileged to be included among her students and I appreciate her generous feedback on my work.

Others have given me valuable advice and support on this project. Robin Moremen served as my sounding board throughout the research and writing process. Maria Carrig, Catherine Cramton and Marie Magleby have been a constant source of encouragement, first as a dissertation support group and now during monthly encounters over electronic mail. Michael Musheno offered insightful comments on early ideas. I thank Roxanne Elings and Tom Haynie for the use of their Manhattan apartment while conducting interviews for this project. Keith Chrzan and Bill Cunningham gave me statistical advice. Thanks to Chris Lenko, Kerry Rockquemore, Paul Magro and Mark Chaves for commenting on various drafts of the manuscript. I am appreciative of Dwight Burlingame and James Wood, Indiana University Center on Philanthropy, for the invitation to publish this book as part of the Governance Series of the Indiana University Press. Thanks to Robert Sloan, sponsoring editor at Indiana University Press. Finally, and most especially, I thank Lois Sherman, Publications Manager at the Center for Philanthropy, for her fine editorial advice and patience.

I have benefited from financial and/or intellectual support from the The National Science Foundation (Grant #SES-9001086), Indiana University Center on Philanthropy (Fellowship in Nonprofit

Governance), Yale University's Program on Nonprofit Organizations (John D. Rockefeller 3rd Graduate Research Fellowship), and the Working Group Conference on Feminist Organizations (Washington, DC, 1992) organized by Patricia Yancey Martin and Myra Marx Ferree. The usual disclaimer applies: I take full responsibility for the ideas presented in this book.

On a more personal note, I'd like to thank my family and friends who have been instrumental in helping me on my journey. Thanks to Dale and Patricia Bordt, Sharon Dellorto, Mindy Scholten, Robin Moremen, Heather Markette, Chris Lenko, Sarah Mustillo, John Todd, Jody Horn, Debbie Schneider, Katherine Thomas and Catherine Fobes. For their spiritual guidance and unconditional love, I dedicate this book to Claudia Munro, Diane Diver and Marlene Roberts.

INTRODUCTION

This project was inspired by my experience with two nonprofit organizations in Connecticut more than ten years ago. I was involved in the formation of two very different groups. Inside-Out: Citizens United for Prison Reform, Inc., was a grassroots, community-based effort initiated by a former offender and his spouse to educate the public about the conditions of the prison system in Connecticut and to mobilize support for prisoners' rights among ex-offenders, family members, and concerned citizens. The Graduate Feminist Women in the Social Sciences (GFWSS) was a support group and intellectual forum for graduate students at Yale University who were engaged in feminist research and writing in various social science disciplines. I was struck by the contrast between the initial meetings of Inside-Out and the initial gatherings of GFWSS.

In the case of Inside-Out, the ex-offender and his spouse set a date for a public forum to discuss the possibility of starting an organization. The word was spread through a newsletter they had been writing and distributing for more than a year. About 25 people showed up at the first meeting, which was held in Hartford. Within two hours, the group was formed. Using majority vote, we decided on the organization's name, officers (president, vice president, secretary and treasurer) and drafted a mission statement. We prioritized a list of tasks that needed to be done and delegated these tasks to various committees. A month later at the second meeting, without any discussion, the meeting was conducted by the president using Robert's Rules of Order. The organization's bylaws (which were drafted by one of the committees) and the mission statement were voted on and approved.

About the same time, a group of seven female graduate students at Yale were commiserating over dinner. We were all working on feminist projects (of various sorts) and were feeling isolated from each other and estranged from the faculty because there were so few female faculty role models at the time (and even fewer feminists). We decided that we needed to start networking across disciplines in the social sciences to combat our feeling of isolation. We also wanted to bring in feminist scholars from the outside to quench our thirst for direction and support from established, academic women. The group met for a couple of weeks, talking strategy before we decided to have an open meeting. Posters were placed around campus advertising the first gathering. The meeting drew approximately 30 women from sociology, political science, organizational behavior, American studies, economics, and psychology. Unlike the experience with Inside-Out, very little was decided in that first open meeting of GFWSS. In fact, over the next several meetings we talked primarily about organizational process and very little about content. We asked ourselves the following questions: How should meetings be conducted? How do we insure that one person or a few people don't dominate the decision-making process? What do we do with "natural" leaders and "natural" followers? Do we close the organization to newcomers at some point to promote cohesiveness? How do we make sure that students from all social science disciplines feel welcome? After much discussion and debate, we decided to have a rotating facilitator for each meeting and a rotating record keeper to enhance equal participation. Decisions would be made by consensus. We decided to keep the membership open to newcomers for the sake of inclusiveness. Many of these issues about the organization's structure were revisited periodically over the next several months, and adjustments were made.

I asked myself why my initial experiences in these two organizations were so different. Inside-Out was not explicitly concerned with its organizational structure. In fact, we adopted a traditional, hierarchical model without discussion during the first session. GFWSS, in contrast, was overly concerned with the structure of the group. We agonized for weeks over questions of leadership, division of labor and inclusiveness of membership. Was the difference related to the fact that GFWSS was a feminist organization and Inside-Out was not? If this had been the 1960s, my response probably would have been yes. (Although I was too young to have participated, I had read extensively about feminist collectives during the early years of the contemporary women's movement.) But this was 1986. Wasn't the debate about organizational structure over? Weren't women more open to a range of organizational forms? In fact, didn't many women's organizations now endorse bureaucratic structures? Why the continued preoccupation with structure? Was GFWSS living in a time warp? If so, why?

These questions percolated for a year or so while I sat in two seminars on organizational theory. It became clear to me during those courses, and subsequently in the process of studying for my comprehensive examination in organizational theory, that very little empirical research had been done on feminist organizations from an organizational perspective. It was then that I knew I wanted to explore the issue of organizational structure among women's organizations more fully. The purpose of this book is to describe what contemporary women's nonprofit organizations look like structurally and, using organizational theory, explain why they adopt the particular form that they do.

The Study

Women's nonprofit organizations established during the contemporary women's movement (1967-1988) in the five boroughs of New York City constitute the focus of this study. Although the specific details of the research methodology can be found in the Appendix, I want to make a few preliminary remarks here. New York

City was selected as my research site because it was one of the major centers of feminist activism during the early years of the contemporary women's movement and continues to be the home of a large number of women's organizations. New York City is also close to New Haven, Connecticut, where I was living at the time, and the proximity facilitated my field work (the train ride from New Haven to Grand Central Station is roughly 90 minutes). In the beginning, I used a combination of national and local directories of women's organizations, mailing lists of existing organizations, local feminist periodicals, feminist newspapers, and feminist newsletters to identify all the women's nonprofit organizations in the city. Using specific selection criteria, I arrived at a population of nearly 200 women's nonprofit organizations.

The primary source of data for this study is a self-administered questionnaire mailed to each organization and completed by the director or spokeswoman for the organization. Employing Dillman's (1978) "Total Design Method" for mail surveys, I ended up with 113 completed questionnaires, which is a 57 percent response rate. The quantitative analyses presented in the book are based on these survey data. Subsequent to the collection of the quantitative data, I conducted interviews with members of a sample of organizations that completed the survey (n=30), kept field notes of my trip to each interview site and of the physical setting of the organization, and analyzed organizational documents (such as brochures, newsletters, employee handbooks, and mission statements) provided by the organizations. These qualitative data are introduced throughout the book to add texture and nuance to the quantitative analysis. At each stage of data collection, I assured the participants in my study that their identities, as well as the names of their organizations, would remain anonymous. Therefore, I use pseudonyms for the organizations throughout the book.

An Outline of the Book

Chapter 1 locates my research question in the debates about organizational structure that took place among feminists involved in the early years of the contemporary women's movement. I establish that early second-wave feminists were preoccupied with the form, or structure, that their organizations adopted. And, I consider why we might anticipate a shift away from such a preoccupation today, given recent research on women's organizations.

Chapters 2 and 3 are concerned with the question "What do women's nonprofit organizations look like?" I begin in Chapter 2 with a descriptive overview of the population of organizations used in this study. Then, I operationalize a long-standing conceptual framework for understanding organizational form and illustrate the ideal typical forms (bureaucracy and collectives) using qualitative data from two organizations. In Chapter 3 I develop a typology of women's nonprofits that captures the full range of variation in structure that exists among the organizations in this study. The majority of women's organizations in New York City are hybrid organizations of two kinds—what I have termed "professional organizations" and "pragmatic collectives." A small number resemble conventional bureaucracy, and an even smaller number are collectivist in pure form. Although the presence of the two hybrid forms is not a surprise, I did not expect them to represent the majority of women's nonprofits. Documenting the prevalence of hybrids and detailing the exact structural configuration of each is a major contribution of this research.

Chapter 4 shifts to the question of why women's nonprofits in New York City look the way that they do. Does ideology drive form? Is form determined by the nature of the work an organization does? Is organizational structure dependent on whom a group interacts with in the outside world? Or are size and age what matter? I argue that the answer is different for bureaucracies and collectives compared to hybrid organizational forms. Age, ideology and tasks are the best predictors of bureaucratic and collectivist organizations. Size, organizational constituency and "networking as core work" best predict hybrids. I consider the implications these findings have for both organizational theory and research on women's organizations in Chapter 5.

Two Narratives

Although the core of the book centers on survey data, qualitative data are important in that they add narrative to the numbers. I introduce two such narratives here. New Beginnings and Women with Hardhats, fictitious names for two women's nonprofits in New York City, will be revisited throughout the book.

New Beginnings

New Beginnings is a women's nonprofit organization in a borough of New York City. It began in 1980 as a program within a larger human service organization to help battered women in the community, particularly ethnic minority women with special needs. Today, New Beginnings consists of a shelter system of 35 beds in separate apartments and a center for counseling, child care, job referral, and advocacy. Twelve full-time staff provide services to between 25 and 50 women and children every month. New Beginnings is funded primarily by the city government and is a member of a number of local and regional task forces on domestic violence.

My journey to New Beginnings sheds light on the organization and its environment. The train (and subsequent cab) trip from Grand Central Station took an hour and a half, as New Beginnings is located on a peninsula in South Queens. Near the end of the ride, the train came up from underground and traveled along the water. The contrast between the gorgeous, beach-like terrain lining the water and the stark, dilapidated buildings scattered throughout was striking.

I was uncomfortable getting off the train when it stopped. I was the only Anglo for as far as I could see, and I became very conscious of my whiteness. I was reminded of how isolated I was from the real world as a graduate student, even in racially diverse New Haven. The taxi stand was hidden across the street, through a lot filled with cars that were either abandoned or being worked on. I walked up to the man at the office, and he told me to wait for the cab outside. An unmarked, rusted-out car pulled up and the man inside stared at me. It wasn't until I walked up to the car that I saw a cab radio on the dash and knew for sure it was my ride.

During the drive, I learned that the community is populated with an interesting mix of African-Americans and Orthodox Jews. Spaced between blocks of run-down houses was the occasional, very elaborately designed synagogue. Prior to a disastrous real estate bust in the 1920s, the community was a resort area for the middle-class. After several failed attempts at urban renewal, much of what remains today is a squalid slum.

New Beginnings is located in what looks like an old warehouse with loading docks on one side. I was told ahead of time to go to the back and up a flight of stairs. This was easier said than done. It was difficult to tell which side was the back. And the taxi driver was of little help. Dropping me off in the middle of the parking lot, he said, "This is where I let off people who give me this address." Fortunately, a man unloading a dairy truck showed me where to find the back door. The last leg of my trip required that I duck under dripping water to pass through the door and climb a flight of rickety stairs.

New Beginnings is a big open space that is crowded with old furniture, boxes, and ineptly stacked books. On one side of the room was a series of makeshift cubicles. In the center of the room was the director's desk, partially outlined with yellowing Plexiglas and cluttered with stacks of papers, files, dirty coffee mugs, phone books, directories and a marked-up calendar. I sat in an old, overstuffed chair with floral upholstery and waited for the director to finish her conversation with another woman.

Women with Hardhats

Women with Hardhats is a nonprofit organization that provides training and advocacy for disadvantaged women seeking work in the construction industry and other blue-collar trades. It was founded in 1978 as a small project with a single government grant. Today, it is a growing and diversified organization with a full and part-time staff of roughly 14 and a clientele of between 50 and 75 women per month. With a budget of over a million dollars, it receives its funding from both the public and private sector. Women with Hardhats is deeply enmeshed in the women's community in New York City, working collaboratively with a large network of women's organizations in the area.

Women with Hardhats is located in a neighborhood that is considered part of midtown Manhattan, a patchwork of town houses, tenements, luxury apartments and factories. Urban renewal in this area began in the 1950s and 1960s, uprooting large sections of slum housing and rehabilitating the brick and brownstone town houses. The Women with Hardhats building, itself, underwent restoration in the late 1980s.

Women with Hardhats is easily accessible by subway: one stop from Penn Station and a 15-minute ride with transfer from Grand Central. The street itself is quiet relative to the bustle of the people and traffic in the surrounding area. As I approached the building, I was struck by the prominence of the name of the organization and the universal symbol for "women" on the sign above the door. It seemed refreshingly out of place on a street otherwise occupied by parked cars, an occasional delivery truck, and small clusters of African-American men sitting on front stoops.

As I entered the door, I introduced myself to the receptionist and was invited to wait in a chair positioned in front of the window. The reception area was bright, with modern furnishings. The blonde hardwood floors gleamed in the sunlight. As I soon discovered, the upstairs was an open loft-like space equally light and cheery. Off to one side was a large work table surrounded by comfortable chairs. Near the back of the room were three desks attractively arranged with lamps, chairs, and common workspaces.

As you will learn in Chapter 2, New Beginnings and Women with Hardhats represent a typical collectivist organization and a typical bureaucratic organization, respectively. I eventually argue that collectivist and bureaucratic forms of organization are rare among the women's nonprofits in this study. The story, however, begins with these two ideal types.

1

THE DEBATE ABOUT ORGANIZATIONAL FORM IN THE CONTEMPORARY WOMEN'S MOVEMENT

Internally...we proceed in a collective spirit which encourages self-criticism, individual self-determination and initiative, and non-competitiveness... An organization can be said to move collectively only when leadership is encouraged in each member, and trust is placed in individual as well as collective judgment.
—Official statement of a women's organization, 1971

I'd say all the high-level staff here hold very conventional views of management. We're here to get the job done, not to talk about the warm fuzzy stuff... The issue of organizational structure is raised now and then by young women in the office who didn't go through all those discussions in the sixties. But most of us want to get on with the work.
—Member of a women's organization, 1991

As the first quote above suggests, women activists paid a great deal of attention to the issue of organizational form when setting up groups in the early years of the contemporary women's movement in the United States.[1] How a group was structured was just as important as what the group set out to accomplish. Collectivism was promoted as the ideal form of organization. The second quote, voiced twenty years later, takes a different position. Not only has the focus on organizational structure subsided, but more conventional organizational forms are viewed as quite acceptable. Are these two quotes representative of a more general shift in thinking among women creating and operating organizations today? The purpose of this book is to answer this question by describing the organizational structure of a large number of contemporary women's organizations. Focusing on the population of women's nonprofit organizations founded in New York City between 1967 and 1988, I document what these organizations look like structurally and explain why they adopt a particular form. In doing so, I argue that women have moved beyond their original preoccupation with organizational form, which often took the form of denigrating bureaucracy and romanticizing collectives. Rather than pitting bureaucracy against collectives, women today are creating hybrid forms of organization that combine, in innovative ways, the best characteristics of both.

Early Debates Over Organizational Form

The early discussions about organizational structure were of two kinds. First, women articulated what was wrong with adopting conventional, bureaucratic structures. Some claimed there exists a fundamental incompatibility between bureaucracy and feminism (Browne 1976; Kornegger 1975; Rothschild 1976). Bureaucracy embodies a masculine ethic that fails to reflect and is antithetical to female experience and values. Whereas bureaucracy relies on hierarchic relations and a division of labor, feminism strives for egalitarian relations and holistic work roles. While bureaucratic power implies domination and coercion, feminists conceptualize power as "empowerment," as the ability to mobilize resources and as collective energy, strength and initiative. Bureaucracies are means to an end; feminists envision organizations as both means and ends (that is, the process should have value). Bureaucracy requires a separation between the public and private spheres of life; feminist definitions of the personal as political, and rationality as the connection between emotion and reason, demand an integration of the two realms. Writing in the late 1970s, Joan Rothschild (1976) illustrates this position:

> The bureaucratic form is both microcosm and blueprint for the way in which modern industrial and post-industrial nations function. Because it perpetuates systems of dominance, creates and depends on elitism, and fosters—indeed glorifies—alienation, obedience, and authoritarianism, bureaucracy must no longer serve as our model. What feminists learn from examining the bureaucratic structure is that form cannot be divorced from content, and that what we call form must be as important to our future society goals as the content of our program. (p. 28)

Second, drawing on their experience in the civil rights movement and the new left, women developed an alternative way of organizing. Specifically, they espoused a collectivist ideal and worked to translate collectivism into organizational practice (Evans 1979; Freeman 1974; O'Sullivan 1976; Ware 1970). Collectivism consists of the following characteristics:

1. Authority is distributed among all members;
2. Leadership is a temporary role assumed by each member through the rotation of chair or facilitator position;
3. Decision making is participatory;
4. Division of labor is minimal and specific tasks are rotated among individuals;
5. Information, resources, and rewards are equally shared among all;
6. Power is conceptualized as empowerment rather than domination;
7. The process of organization is as valuable as the outcome; and
8. Social relations are based on personal, communal, and holistic ideals (Rothschild-Whitt 1979).

Women set up a wide range of organizations that were based on these collectivist principles. Many began as consciousness-raising groups and later developed into for-profit and nonprofit services, including coffee houses, women's shelters, bookstores, food co-ops, health centers, legal clinics, liberation schools, rape crisis centers, and publishing houses (Ferree & Hess 1994; Freeman 1975; Woodul 1984).

Most of the concern over organizational form was among women in only one strand of the early women's movement: the younger, more radical feminists. This emphasis on collectivism, however, influenced the mainstream strand of the movement by forcing the older women to enter the debate over organizational form, even if it was in defense of bureaucracy. In some cases the influence was more profound. There have been instances where the younger strand of activists convinced the older women of the merits of collectivism. For example, conventionally structured groups such as the National Organization for Women (NOW) began to incorporate collectivist ideas, such as the free expression of ideas and emotions, into their organizations (Carden 1974; Ferguson 1984). So, even though early activists never reached consensus on the virtues of collectivism, the concern over organizational structure dominated movement discussions, writings, and practices from the late 1960s through the 1970s (Carden 1974; Echols 1989; Ferree & Hess 1994; Freeman 1975; Martin 1990; Matthews 1994).

As the women's movement matured, what happened to this preoccupation with organizational form? Does structure continue to take a high priority among women creating groups? Is there still intense rhetoric against bureaucracy? What has happened to women's organizations in practice? Do women's organizations continue to favor collectivist structures? Are they successful at maintaining them? Based on recent research on women's organizations, we have some hint that women's concern over organizational structure has changed with time. The next section is a brief review of recent research.

Recent Research on Women's Organizations

Recent research on women's organizations suggests a change in thinking about organizational structure. First, social histories of the contemporary women's movement have documented how organizational form has been replaced by organizational strategy as a defining factor among women's movement organizations (Ferree & Hess 1994; Ryan 1992). Second, theoretical discussions of feminist organizations encourage women to be more discriminating among organizational structures, rather than uncritically assuming that collectivist structures are the only ones consistent with feminist ideology. For example, Mansbridge (1984) argues that feminists should not take the position that there is only one "form of freedom." Rather, the structures women adopt for their organizations should depend on the context. Martin (1990) encourages us to move away from using organizational structure as the way of defining what constitutes a feminist organization, arguing that excessive attention has been given to organizational structure (particularly the dichotomy between bureaucracy and collectives), to the exclusion of other defining factors such as feminist values, goals, outcomes, and practices.

Third, based on empirical studies of women's organizations, it is clear that some women have taken a more moderate position by adopting hybrid organizational forms, which blend aspects of both bureaucracy and collectives. For instance, Gottfried and Weiss (1994) find evidence of what they call a "compound feminist organization" in their case study of Purdue University's Council on the Status of Women. One of the political advantages of such a hybrid form is its ability to accommodate membership diversity. Based on research on three feminist organizations, Iannello (1992) uncovered the use of "modified consensus," a structural invention that allows for decisions to be made without a reliance on hierarchy or pure consensus. Leidner (1991) documents the unique structural innovations of the National Women's Studies Association, which were a product of the group's desire to reconcile collectivist principles and inclusiveness. Finally, in a study of the battered women's movement in Texas, Reinelt (1994; 1995) shows how the boundaries are blurred between hierarchical and collective processes in battered women's movement organizations.

Despite these suggestive findings, we do not know what has happened regarding organizational structure based on a systematic assessment of a large group of women's organizations in a particular locale. Here rests the impetus behind, and purpose of, this book.

2

WHAT DO WOMEN'S NONPROFITS LOOK LIKE? CONCEPTUALIZING ORGANIZATIONAL FORM

We have been told by feminist scholars what women's organizations should look like (Ferguson 1984; Freeman 1974; Mansbridge 1984). And through case studies, we know how some women's nonprofits actually look (for example, Barnett 1995; Brown 1992; Iannello 1992; Leidner 1991; Rodriguez 1988; Staggenborg 1989). But we have little knowledge about the broader empirical terrain and variation in women's nonprofit organizations. I describe that sector in one major urban setting and, in doing so, make two primary contributions. First, in this chapter, I operationalize a long-standing conceptual framework for understanding organizational form (that is, Rothschild-Whitt 1979). Second, in Chapter 3, I use cluster analysis to develop a typology of women's nonprofits that captures the range of variation in structure that exists among them. I begin with a description of the population of organizations.

Overview

Women's nonprofit organizations in New York City can be described in terms of their focus, scope, size, age, organizational philosophy and source of funding. What becomes clear from such a description is that the groups in the study represent a diverse sector of organizational life.

Focus of Activities and Services

Nonprofit organizations set up by women and for women in New York City are involved in a variety of services and activities. As Table 2.1 indicates, thirteen service and advocacy areas are represented among the 113 organizations that returned completed questionnaires for this study. Twenty-one percent of the groups are concerned with numerous issues relevant to the lives of women; I have labeled these "multi-issue" organizations. Seventy-nine percent primarily concentrate their

TABLE 2.1
Type of Organization

Type of Organization	N	Percent
Multi-issue	24	21
Health (services and education)	15	13
Education	10	9
Employment	10	9
Women's Centers (community and college-based)	11	10
Rape Crisis	10	9
Politics	7	6
Counseling	7	6
Domestic Violence	7	6
Legal Advocacy/ Criminal Justice	7	6
Homeless	3	3
Child care	1	1
Religious	1	1
Total	113	100

efforts around one particular area, such as health services, education, or employment. While most of the organizations target their efforts toward all women, thirty-three percent of the groups explicitly advocate for or provide services to minority populations, including ethnic and racial minorities (twenty-one organizations), lesbians and gay men (eleven organizations), older women (four groups), and disabled women (one organization).

Scope, Size, and Age

The organizations are varied in terms of their scope as well. Table 2.2 displays the number of groups that are international, national, statewide, and community-based, as well as the number of groups that are situated within a larger organization (for example, a rape crisis center in a hospital, a women's center in a university). Within each of these categories, there are groups providing direct services to clients, membership organizations, membership organizations that provide services, and advocacy organizations that do not provide direct services or have a formal membership. Sixty-nine percent of the organizations have at least one paid staff person. The remaining thirty-one percent are strictly volunteer associations.

Many of the groups are small in terms of the number of full-time working members. For example, sixty-eight percent have five or fewer

TABLE 2.2
Type of Organization

Scope of Organization	N	Percent
International	6	5
National headquarters	14	12
National branch	15	13
State-level	4	4
Community-based	42	38
Unit or department	32	28
Total	113	100

full-time working members (including staff, officers, governing board members, and volunteers). Yet, it is clear that the impact of these organizations is far-reaching. Of those offering direct services, sixty-nine percent serve more than fifty women per month. And, among the membership organizations, sixty percent have a membership of over fifty individuals.

Finally, the organizations in this study were founded during various stages of the contemporary women's movement. As Table 2.3 shows, twenty-one percent were over seventeen years old at the time of study, having been established during the period 1967-1973. Thirty-seven percent emerged during the consolidation of the movement (1974-1979), and forty-two percent are the product of the 1980s. Of those founded in the 1980s, eleven percent are relatively young organizations (five years old or less at the time this study was conducted).

TABLE 2.3
Date of Foundation

Years	N	Percent
1967-1973	22	21
1974-1979	40	37
1980-1984	33	31
1985-1988	12	11
Total	107	100

missing cases=6

Philosophy

The philosophies that inform these groups are as diverse as their substantive focus, scope, and age. As Table 2.4 demonstrates, slightly over one half (fifty-five percent) of the groups consider themselves *feminist* organizations either in membership or purpose.[1] Feminism takes on different meanings for those who adopt this philosophy. The range of definitions includes "working for women's equality," "believing women and men are different but equal," "the empowerment of all women and the end of oppression on the basis of sex, race, class,

TABLE 2.4
Organizational Philosophy

Does Your Group Consider Itself A Feminist Organization?	N	Percent
Yes	62	55
Subject has not come up	27	24
No	15	14
Unresolved	8	7
Total	112	100

missing cases=1

sexual orientation," "total liberation for all," and a "woman-identified focus on all issues affecting all inhabitants of this planet and the planet itself."

There are also important distinctions to make among the remaining organizations that do not adopt a feminist philosophy. For the fifty organizations (forty-five percent of the total population) that do not consider themselves feminists, fifteen groups (fourteen percent of total) explicitly reject feminism, eight groups (seven percent of total) have not resolved whether they do or do not have a feminist philosophy, and the issue of feminism has never come up for twenty-seven (twenty-four percent of the total) of these women's groups.

The first two possibilities (that is, why organizations might reject feminism or be unresolved over the issue) are understandable. And when I probed further, the explanations women gave were consistent with what I imagined. For example, most suggested that feminism is too narrow a concept or too exclusionary for their goals, which include a wider target population than women (for example, people of color; lesbians and gay men; or in some service areas, all victims—not women exclusively). When asked what alternative philosophies guide their organization, only a few specified their orientation: humanistic, human rights, self-help.

The latter finding (that is, feminism never coming up), is more difficult to interpret. How could a group of women organized for women not at least *consider* whether feminism had anything to do with their work or cause? Wouldn't they have to work pretty hard to prevent such a discussion from surfacing? A variety of types of organizations are represented among the groups for which feminism has never come up for discussion (for example, community centers, counseling, domestic violence, general, health education, employment, politics). Yet, they are similar in two respects. The organizations are either engaged in direct service delivery and/or are groups that target minority populations (women of color, lesbians and gay men). It is conceivable that the former *assume* a social service orientation and see themselves as apolitical, therefore eliminating the possibility of discussing other philosophies or politics at all. For the latter, because feminism has historically been viewed as a white, middle-class movement of women, it also makes sense that when women of color come together, feminism is not among the range of philosophies with which the group members identify, debate over, and overtly accept or reject.

Sources of Funding

As one would expect, the majority of organizations (seventy-seven percent) rely on more than one source of funding. Table 2.5 ranks each funding source according to the frequency with which they contribute (either in whole or part) to the support of the groups in this study. For example, fifty-seven percent of the organizations are sustained (in whole or part) through individual contributions. In contrast, only six percent of the groups (in whole or part) are supported by churches or synagogues.

When the funding sources are grouped according to individual (that is, individual contributions, fundraising events, membership dues, service fees) versus organizational sources (foundations, government, parent organization, businesses or corporations, churches or synagogues), I find that fifty-four percent of the organizations get the majority of their funding from organizational sources, forty percent are primarily supported by individual funding sources, and six percent receive half their resources from organizations and half from individuals (see Table 2.6).

TABLE 2.5
Rank Order of Funding Sources
(Organizations funded, in whole or part, by each source)

Rank	Source	N	Percent
1	Individual contributions	62	57
2	Fundraising events	46	43
3	Foundations	43	40
4	State/federal government	40	37
5	Membership dues	36	33
6	Service fees	31	29
7	Parent organization	19	18
8	Local government	17	16
8	Businesses/corporations	17	16
10	Churches/synagogues	6	6

missing cases=5

TABLE 2.6
Distribution of Individual Versus
Organizational Sources of Funding

Source	N	Percent
Organizational (51-100 percent)	58	54
Individual (51-100 percent)	43	40
Both (50 percent org/ 50 percent ind)	7	6
Total	108	100

missing cases=5

Organizational Structure

Because bureaucracy is the primary organizational form in modern society, organizations that have nonbureaucratic structures are generically referred to by organizational scholars as alternative organizations, or collectives. I use the contrast between bureaucracies and collectives as a conceptual starting point in anticipating the structure of women's organizations in the nonprofit sector.

Bureaucracy and Collectives as Ideal Types

The study of bureaucracy as a major line of sociological inquiry originates in the work of Max Weber, a German sociologist, who wrote on the origins, characteristics, and consequences of bureaucracy around the turn of this century (Weber 1978, vols. 1 and 2). While Weber's insights on bureaucracy are many and far-reaching, the features of bureaucracy as a distinct organizational form are what concern me.

Weber's conception of bureaucracy consists of several key elements. Bendix (1968) outlines Weber's definition of bureaucracy as follows:

> According to Weber, a bureaucracy establishes a relation between legally instated authorities and their subordinate officials which is characterized by defined rights and duties, prescribed in written regulations; authority relations between positions, which are ordered systematically; appointment and promotion based on contractual agreements and regulated accordingly; technical training or experience as a formal condition of employment; fixed monetary salaries; a strict separation of office and incumbent in the sense that the official does not own the means of administration and cannot appropriate the position; and administrative work as a full-time occupation. (206)

Weber presents his definition of bureaucracy as an ideal type, which is a simplification and an exaggeration of what we find in the empirical world. Weber, himself, referred to ideal types as one-sided accentuations of reality. By developing ideal types, we gain conceptual clarity of an otherwise complex phenomenon. In introducing Weber's work, Rhinestein (1954) claims the following about Weber's ideal conception of bureaucracy:

Situations of such pure type have never existed in history… The ideal types of Weber's sociology are simply mental constructs to serve as categories of thought, the use of which will help us to catch the infinite manifoldness of reality. (xxix-xxx)

In addition to being simplifications for clarity's sake, ideal types can be viewed as models containing hypotheses to be empirically tested (see Giddens 1982:202-203). The question becomes: To what extent does Weber's model of bureaucracy predict what we will find in the empirical world? For instance, actual bureaucratic organizations may contain only a few of the structural properties identified by Weber, or the characteristics may exist in varying degrees.

While clearly the dominant form of organization, bureaucracy is not the only type. Moreover, it is commonly recognized today that bureaucracy is not unidimensional. Rothschild-Whitt offers an ideal type of collectivist organization that is in direct contrast to bureaucracy. She identifies eight dimensions that differentiate collectives from bureaucracy.[2] There are, of course, other ways to think about organizations than in terms of dimensions of bureaucracy (or collectivism). Because feminist debates over organizational form historically have centered on bureaucracy and collectives, however, I will maintain this focus here.

Table 2.7 summarizes Rothschild-Whitt's conceptualization of each dimension that distinguishes bureaucracy from collectives. The first dimension, authority, refers to who is responsible for making key organizational decisions, ranging from the members of the organization as a group to an individual in her capacity as officeholder. According to Rothschild-Whitt, the greater the reliance on an individual officeholder to make key decisions, the more bureaucratic the organization. Conversely, the greater the reliance on the members of the organization as a group to make major decisions, the more collectivist the organization.

Rules have to do with the number, specificity, and use of formal, written rules and regulations in actual decision making. The greater the number, the greater the specificity, and the greater the use of formal rules, the more bureaucratic the organization. The fewer, the less

TABLE 2.7
Rothschild - Whitt's Two Ideal Types of Organization

Dimensions	Bureaucratic Organizations	Collectivist Organizations
Authority	Authority resides in individuals by virtue of incumbency in office and/or expertise; hierarchical organization of offices.	Authority resides in the collectivity as a whole; delegated, if at all, only temporarily and subject to recall.
Rules	Formalization of fixed and universalistic rules.	Minimal stipulated rules; primacy of ad hoc individuated decisions.
Social control	Behavior is subject to social control, through supervision or standardized rules and sanctions.	Social controls are primarily based on personalistic or moralistic appeals.
Social relations	Ideal of impersonality. Relations are role-based, segmental, and instrumental.	Ideal of community. Relations are holistic, personal, and of value in themselves.
Recruitment and advancement	Employment based on specialized training and formal certification. Advancement based on seniority or achievement.	Employment based on friends, social-political values, personality, and informally assessed knowledge and skills. Advancement not meaningful as there is no hierarchy of positions.
Incentive structure	Remunerative incentives are primary.	Normative and solidarity incentives are primary; material incentives are secondary.
Social stratification	Differential rewards; hierarchy justifies inequality.	Egalitarian distribution of rewards.
Differentiation	Maximal specialization of jobs and functions; segmental roles.	Generalization of jobs and functions; holistic roles.

Rothschild-Whitt, Joyce. 1979. "The Collectivist Organization: An Alternative to Rational-Bureaucratic Models." *American Sociological Review* 44:509-527.

specific, and the less used the rules, the more the organization lies at the collectivist end of the continuum.

Third, social control involves the presence of formal control mechanisms, the presence of methods of informal control, particularly homogeneity of membership, and use of formal versus informal means of control in actual decision making. The greater the number of formal control mechanisms, the more heterogeneous the membership, and the greater the use of formal means of control in decision making, the more bureaucratic the organization. In contrast, the fewer the formal controls, the more homogeneous the membership, and the less the use of formal control in decision making, the more collectivist the organization.

Social relations vary by degree of impersonality among organizational members and are measured by the extent to which organizational members spend time together outside the organization and the degree to which members consider each other friends. The more members confine their interactions to the work setting and the more instrumental their relationships with coworkers, the more bureaucratic the organization; the less these are true, the more collectivist the organization.

For Rothschild-Whitt, recruitment and advancement refer to the kind of criteria that are used in selecting individuals for organizational membership and for promotion. Criteria range from being political or subjective to objective. The more objective the recruitment and advancement criteria, the more bureaucratic the organization. The more political or subjective the criteria, the more collectivist the organization.

The sixth dimension, incentive structure, is concerned with the types of organizational inducements or rewards that are meaningful to organizational participants, ranging from normative to material. The greater the emphasis on material incentives, the more bureaucratic the group; the greater the emphasis on normative incentives, the more collectivist the organization.

Social stratification involves the extent to which monetary rewards are distributed equally or unequally among organizational members. The greater the differences in pay among members, the more bureaucratic the organization. The more similar the pay among members, the more collectivist the organization.

Last, differentiation refers to the division of labor in the organization, measured in terms of the number of distinct job titles and the permanency of these jobs. The more job titles and the greater extent to which the jobs are permanent, the more bureaucratic the organization; the reverse is characteristic of collectives.

Despite the conceptualization of bureaucracy and collectives as ideal types, in the real world, it is quite conceivable that organizations may vary substantially along each of the eight dimensions. Early attempts to measure bureaucracy empirically substantiate this idea (Hall 1963; Pugh et al. 1968; Udy 1959). For example, Stanley Udy was among the first to reformulate Weber's ideal type of bureaucracy as a model in order to assess empirically the extent to which the elements of bureaucracy were associated with one another in real organizations. He found that the characteristics of bureaucracy vary from their pure form and that the characteristics do not necessarily vary in the same way or same direction. Richard Hall's (1963) work is another example. Based on a diverse sample of U.S. organizations, he found that the dimensions of bureaucracy vary independently of one another.

Matching the Ideal Types to the Real World of Women's Organizations

In order to describe the organizational structure of contemporary women's nonprofits in New York City, I first operationalized the eight dimensions proposed by Rothschild-Whitt (1979), creating forty-six measures of organizational form. Next, I conducted an exploratory factor analysis to examine the underlying patterns or relationships that exist for these forty-six variables (Hair et al. 1984).[3] I turn to the results of this analysis now.

The analysis resulted in the seven factors presented in Table 2.8.[4] Organizations that fall on the high end of each of the dimensions are closest to the bureaucratic ideal type; those that fall on the low end resemble the collectivist ideal type. I describe each of the dimensions, illustrating them with examples from New Beginnings and Women with Hardhats. New Beginnings, the organization for battered women,

TABLE 2.8
Dimensions of Organizational Structure
Among Women's Nonprofits in New York City

Dimensions	Bureaucratic Organizations	Collectivist Organizations
Material Incentives & Formal Structures	Importance given to material rewards; permanent job positions; numerous written rules and formal social controls.	Material rewards are secondary; job rotation; few written rules and formal social controls.
Normative Incentives	Normative rewards are secondary.	Importance given to normative rewards (e.g., personal empowerment, effecting social change).
Decision-Making Authority	Individual officeholders make decisions regarding key personnel matters.	Group as a whole makes decisions regarding key personnel matters.
Formal Decision-Making Criteria	Use of written sanctions, disciplinary procedures, and written policy in decision making.	Minimal use of written sanctions, disciplinary procedures, and written policy in decision making.
Shared Beliefs and Time	Members have different political beliefs; rarely spend time together outside work.	Members have similar political beliefs; spend time together outside work.
Informal Decision-Making Criteria	Minimal use of informal criteria (for example, individual judgment, fairness, opinion of group) in decision making.	Use of informal criteria (e.g., individual judgment, fairness, opinion of group) in decision making.
Differentiation	Numerous distinct job positions; economic and educational diversity among members.	Few distinct job positions; economic and educational similarity among members.

is structured collectively; Women with Hardhats, the organization for women seeking employment in the construction industry, is bureaucratic in form.

The first dimension of organizational structure I have named "Material Incentives and Formal Structures." This includes material incentives (such as wages or salaries, vacation and time off, opportunities for promotion, and health insurance), the permanency of the job position, the number of written rules (for example, job descriptions, written policies) and the number of formal social controls (for example, disciplinary procedures, performance evaluations). This means that organizations emphasizing material incentives also fill jobs on a permanent basis, have many written rules, and have many formal controls.

Women with Hardhats falls on the bureaucratic end of this dimension. The most important incentives that drive the women in this organization are salaries, health insurance, child care, time-off, and opportunities for promotion. This is consistent with the mission of the organization: advancing the position and conditions for women who are seeking employment in nontraditional fields. Additionally, in Women with Hardhats, all the full- and part-time positions are permanent ones. They have highly specified written rules, including job descriptions, personnel procedure manuals, program policies and organizational by-laws. When it comes to internal social controls, again, Women with Hardhats has a number of formal mechanisms, such as performance evaluations, disciplinary procedures, other written rules outlining how to handle misconduct, and employee grievance procedures.

In contrast, New Beginnings lies on the other, more collectivist, end of this dimension. Material incentives, such as wages, promotions, and the like, are not major motivations for those who work with battered women in this setting. While, technically, all the job positions are permanent, there is a lot of job sharing and "filling in" when the need arises. For example, it is not uncommon for the director to fill in as a caseworker for a day or the bookkeeper to assume the office manager's position if someone is out sick, on vacation, or wants to learn a new aspect of the organization. While New Beginnings does have some written rules and formal social control mechanisms on the books, they are few and nonspecific. The ones they do have are generated by their parent organization and are proposed only as guidelines. For the most part, the various programs within the larger organization (New Beginnings being one) are given a lot of latitude in deciding whether or not to adopt similar written rules. New Beginnings has chosen the informal route when it comes to operations.

The second dimension represents "Normative Incentives," which includes challenging/interesting work, opportunity to effect social change, shared purpose among coworkers, chances to use skills, personal empowerment, and friendships with coworkers. Organizations that value challenging work roles also tend to value the other normative incentives listed above. Women with Hardhats echoes other bureaucratic organizations in downplaying these kinds of work incentives. Like the clients they serve, the women who work here are striving to achieve equity between women and men in the workplace, and usually measures of equity focus on material, not normative, rewards. New Beginnings, on the other hand, places great value on the nonmaterial rewards they get from their work. Achieving recognition in the community, having a shared purpose among coworkers, chances to use skills, and personal empowerment all outrank wages or salaries as important incentives for working at the center. This is consistent with the fairly low range of salaries that the staff make per year, especially in terms of New York City standards: $14,000-$37,000.

An additional dimension of organizational structure is portrayed in "Decision-making Authority." This includes who makes decisions regarding personnel matters (such as requests for leaves of absences, employee discipline, and hiring) and how the organization is stratified by pay. The more an organization relies on individuals (as opposed to committees or the group as a whole) to make decisions, the more likely the organization is stratified in terms of wages and salaries. In Women with Hardhats, key decisions are made by individuals who are responsible for particular areas of the organization. While ultimately accountable to the executive director, there are five directors (director of research and development; director of programs, etc.) who are individually responsible for the decisions made in their area of expertise. In terms of pay, the highest paid employee receives roughly four times the amount of the lowest paid worker. For the most part, in New Beginnings, decision making rests in the hands of the group as a whole, rather than in the hands of the executive director or department heads.[5] And, the pay differential is approximately one half what it is for Women with Hardhats.

The fourth dimension is "Formal Decision-making Criteria" and includes the use of written sanctions, use of disciplinary procedures, and use of written policy. Organizations that rely on written sanctions also often use disciplinary procedures and other written policies. Women with Hardhats relies heavily on the written policies and procedures. In making decisions about hiring new staff, disciplining someone who has engaged in unethical behavior, and granting a leave of absence, formal policy and procedures are at the core of the decision-making process. This is not the case for New Beginnings. Rarely are formal disciplinary procedures or written policy used when making decisions in these three areas.

Dimension five represents "Shared Beliefs and Time." This consists of shared political beliefs (both general and feminist) among organizational members and the extent to which members spend time together outside of work. Those who have similar political views tend to socialize outside the workplace. Members of Women with Hardhats do not necessarily share the same political beliefs or views on feminism. Nor do they spend any meaningful amount of time together outside work. One of the directors put it this way:

> It's a given that what we do here is feminist in nature, so we end up attracting feminist women. Even the two men on staff are conscious of feminist issues. But, we don't put people to a litmus test when we hire them. In fact, we deliberately try to maintain a mix of people on our staff because we work closely with male-dominated industries. You can't impose feminist ideas on these industry people. We just try to convince them that it's in their best interest to hire women and treat them like they do the men (Women with Hardhats, July 31, 1990).

The staff at New Beginnings have similar beliefs and share a fair amount of time together outside the work context. The shared beliefs and time can be best understood in terms of the ethnic context in which the organization is situated—both in terms of its parent organization and the wider community. The parent organization is an ethnic association, and the majority of the staff of New Beginnings have the same ethnic background. Additionally, the community in which this organization is located is isolated from the rest of the borough and has a substantial and close-knit ethnic population.

The sixth dimension is labeled "Informal Decision-making Criteria" and consists of three measures of informal decision making: individual judgment, issues of fairness, and opinions of other members of the group. Those organizations that value individual judgment (rather than strict adherence to rules) also give credence to issues of fairness and the judgments of the group as a whole. These informal criteria rarely enter into the decision-making process at Women with Hardhats. For New Beginnings, however, individual judgment and opinions of other members often play a prominent role in the decision-making process.

"Differentiation" best captures the last dimension. This refers to the number of job titles in an organization, the economic diversity among organizational members, and the educational diversity among organizational members. Organizations that have numerous job positions also employ members with different economic and educational backgrounds. Relative to the other organizations in this study, Women with Hardhats is highly differentiated in terms of the number of distinct job titles that exist and in terms of the diversity in the educational and economic backgrounds of the staff. Not counting volunteers, there are fourteen permanent, paid staff positions. Approximately one half of those who work at Women with Hardhats (including volunteers) have incomes of between $35,000 and $75,000; the remaining half are evenly distributed in two lower income brackets and one higher one. One half of the members have college degrees only, one quarter have high school degrees only, and one quarter have graduate or professional degrees. In contrast, New Beginnings has half as many job titles. The majority of members have incomes of less than $35,000; none makes more than $75,000. Inconsistent with the collectivist ideal, however, there is heterogeneity of educational backgrounds: there is roughly an equal number of members who have less than a high school education, high school degrees only, college only, and graduate/professional degrees.

To summarize, while Rothschild-Whitt's dimensions serve as a useful starting point, my analysis suggests some modification in describing the components of organizational structure for women's nonprofits. The most important adaptation to Rothschild-Whitt's original conceptualization involves two of her dimensions: rules and incentive structures. She suggests that rules vary from informal to formal rules, and that incentives vary from normative to material ones. The data here indicate that an increase in formal rules does not necessarily mean a decrease in informal rules because the two exist on two separate factors (dimensions 4 and 6, respectively). Similarly, an increase in material incentives does not necessarily mean a decrease in normative ones because the two exist on distinct dimensions (dimensions 1 and 2, respectively). It is conceivable, then, that an organizations could score high (or low) on both formal and informal rules and high (or low) on both material and normative incentives. This has important implications for the alternative organizations literature, which implicitly characterizes the formal as "bad" and the informal as "good." In actuality, organizations probably have both and what is either "good" or "bad" is the way in which the organization balances the two to suit its purposes. For example, a battered women's collective that is funded by the government may have lots of formal rules to satisfy their funder's expectations and evaluation procedures. Inside, day-to-day operations, however, may be totally ruled by the informal. Such a scenario is consistent with a version of institutional theory, which I consider in detail in Chapter 4.

We can best summarize the organizational structure of the groups in this study in terms of who makes decisions (Decision-making Authority), how decisions are made (Formal Decision-making Criteria; Informal Decision-making Criteria), how members are related to each other in an official and unofficial sense (Differentiation; Shared Beliefs and Time), and why members participate (Material Incentives and

Formal Structures; Normative Incentives). As we will see in the next chapter, finding the two extreme ends of the organizational continuum (bureaucracy versus collectives) in the real world is rare. Much more frequent are hybrid forms that combine various dimensions of both bureaucracies and collectives. The questions that remain are as follows: If each of these components of structure varies, do they do so in predictable ways? What patterns of variation exist among women's nonprofits in New York City?

3

RARELY BUREAUCRACIES
OR COLLECTIVES:
A TYPOLOGY OF WOMEN'S
NONPROFITS IN NEW YORK CITY

We saw in the previous chapter that the structure of women's organizations in New York City can be described using seven dimensions. Based on previous work (for example, Rothschild-Whitt 1979), I expected to find organizations that represent the two end points of the continuum: bureaucratic organizations and collectivist organizations. Women with Hardhats and New Beginnings illustrate these two end points.

In addition, given the complexity of the real world, it also seemed likely that I would find organizations that fall at various points along the continuum that adopt a combination of both bureaucratic and collectivist characteristics. These have been referred to in the literature as hybrid organizations (see for example, Ferree & Hess 1994; Powell 1987; Staggenborg 1989). For the population of women's nonprofit organizations in New York City, the exact configuration of the hybrids, and thus the number of different kinds of hybrids, is an empirical question. Answering that question is the focus of this chapter.

As Table 3.1 displays, bureaucratic organizations, as an ideal type, score high on the material incentives and formal structure dimension

TABLE 3.1
**Anticipated Variation Among
Organizational Structures**

Organizational Dimension	Organizational Form		
	Bureaucracy	Hybrid	Collective
Material Incentives and Formal Structure	High	High or Low	Low
Normative Incentives	Low	High or Low	High
Decision-making Authority	High	High or Low	Low
Formal Decision-making Criteria	High	High or Low	Low
Shared Beliefs and Time	Low	High or Low	High
Informal Decision-making Criteria	Low	High or Low	High
Differentiation	High	High or Low	Low

and the decision-making authority, formal decision-making criteria, and differentiation dimensions; they score low on the normative incentives, shared beliefs and time, and informal decision-making criteria dimensions. Collectivist organizations follow an opposite pattern, theoretically. They score low on the material incentives and formal structure, decision-making authority, formal decision-making criteria, and differentiation dimensions. Collectives score high on the normative incentives, shared beliefs and time, and informal decision-making criteria dimensions.

In contrast, hybrid organizations should score high on some of the seven dimensions and low on others. As mentioned above, it remains to be seen what specific hybrid patterns will emerge. Given the sheer number of organizations that exist in this context, however, it is likely that at least some of the organizations will fall into this category (or set of categories).

So, how does the empirical reality of women's nonprofit organizations in New York City square with the above expectations? To answer this question I use cluster analysis to describe the variation in organizational forms that exists in this particular setting. Cluster analysis is an analytic technique for categorizing objects or individuals (in this case, organizations) into a small number of meaningful and mutually exclusive subgroups based on similarities among the entities (Hair et al. 1984). The technique is used to identify homogeneous subgroups called "clusters." Here, organizations that are relatively similar on the seven structural dimensions will be grouped together.

Cluster analysis is appropriate when the number of distinct groupings is unknown ahead of time. Although we have some idea about organizational form based on past research, I am interested in finding out how many, and what kind of, clusters will emerge from this particular population of organizations[1]. In this sense, my use of cluster analysis is exploratory.

Based on common sense judgment, and measures of discrimination and reliability (Guerlain 1989), the most meaningful cluster solution consists of four distinct clusters. The technical details explaining how I arrived at this decision are outlined in the Appendix. I have labeled the four clusters bureaucratic, professional, pragmatic collectivist, and collectivist organizations. Clusters 1 (bureaucracies) and 4 (collectives) are consistent with what we expected to find based on past research. Clusters 2 (professional organizations) and 3 (pragmatic collectives) are two different kinds of hybrids. To help you visualize the distribution, Table 3.2 lists the organizations that represent each cluster. For identification purposes, at the beginning of the study each organization was assigned a name and number (for example, Health Education 5). The name refers to the substantive focus of the organization. Within each category (Health Education, Employment, etc.), the organizations were randomly assigned a number.

Below, I briefly describe bureaucratic organizations and collectivist organizations. Then, given that nearly two-thirds of the organizations fall within hybrid categories, I turn to a more detailed description of the two hybrid forms.

Bureaucratic Organizations

Eighteen of the ninety-five organizations (nineteen percent), one of which is Women with Hardhats, typify bureaucracies. As Weber would predict, the empirical organizational reality only approximates

TABLE 3.2
Organization Type by Cluster

Cluster 1: Bureaucratic Organizations (n=18; 19 percent)

Counseling 4	General 4	Health Education 9
Education 9	General 10	Health Services 3
Employment 3	General 12	Health Services 4
Employment 4	General 19	Homeless Shelter 2
*Employment 7	Health Education 2	Law 4
Employment 10	Health Education 5	University Center 1

Cluster 2: Professional Organizations (n=26; 27 percent)

Community Center 2	General 14	Politics 1
Counseling 1	General 22	Politics 3
Counseling 6	Health Education 3	Politics 4
Domestic Violence 1	Health Education 7	Rape 1
Education 5	Health Services 1	Rape 6
Education 7	Health Services 2	#Rape 7
Employment 6	Health Services 6	Rape 9
Employment 8	Homeless Shelter 1	University Center 4
Employment 9	Law 3	

Cluster 3: Pragmatic Collectives (n=43 45 percent)

Childcare 1	Employment 2	Health Services 5
Community Center 3	Employment 5	Law 1
Community Center 4	General 1	Law 2
Counseling 3	General 3	Law 5
Counseling 5	General 5	Rape 2
Counseling 7	General 7	Rape 3
Criminal Justice 2	General 8	Rape 4
Domestic Violence 2	General 11	Rape 5
Domestic Violence 4	General 13	Rape 8
Education 1	General 20	Rape 10
Education 2	General 21	University Center 2
Education 3	Health Education 1	##University Center 6
Education 8	Health Education 4	University Center 7
Education 10	Health Education 6	
Employment 1	Health Education 8	

Cluster 4: Collectivist Organizations (n=8; 8 percent)

Criminal Justice 1	Education 6	Politics 6
Domestic Violence 6	General 17	Religious 1
**Domestic Violence 7	Homeless Shelter 3	

* Women with Hardhats   #City Rape Crisis
**New Beginnings   ##A Space of Her Own

bureaucracy in its ideal-typical form. As Table 3.3 shows, the mean scores for this cluster are high on decision-making authority (which translates into authority resting with an individual officeholder), high on differentiation, low on shared beliefs and time, and low on normative incentives. While we would expect a high score for formal decision-making criteria, a low score for informal decision-making criteria, and a high score for material incentives and formal structure, in actuality this group has middle-range scores on these three dimensions. The bureaucratic cluster represents the largest organizations in the study. The majority of bureaucratic groups have six or more full-time staff.

Collectivist Organizations

Collectivist organizations are the least frequent of the four clusters of organizations. Eight of the ninety-five organizations (eight percent), one of which is New Beginnings, fall within this classification. The characteristics of these organizations are consistent with the theory on collectivist organizations, but they do not replicate a collective in its ideal-typical form. These groups score high on the normative incentives dimension and low on differentiation (see Table 3.3). While we would expect a high score on shared beliefs and time, a high score on informal decision-making criteria, and low scores on the remaining dimensions for a collective in its "pure" form, the data suggest moderate scores instead.

If you recall from Chapter 2, New Beginnings resembled the ideal typical collective to a greater extent than the rest of the organizations in this cluster on average. The exception in the case of New Beginnings was the formal decision-making criteria. If New Beginnings were a "perfect" collective, we would expect to find that decision making rests in the hands of the group as a whole, as opposed to in the hands of the executive director. Consistent with the cluster as a whole, in this case the score is a moderate one. Part of this can be explained in terms of the strong leadership role the executive director has assumed since the days when the center was initially formed. The director went so far as to describe herself as "a little dictatorial," despite the center's overall desire to share in decision making and responsibility.

TABLE 3.3
**Variation in Dimensions of Organizational
Structure by Clusters**

Organizational Dimension	Cluster			
	1 Bureaucratic Organizations	2 Professional Organizations	3 Pragmatic Collectives	4 Collectivist Organizations
Material Incentive and Formal Structure	Medium	Low	Medium	Medium
Normative Incentive	Low	Low	Low	High
Decision–Making Authority	High	Low	Medium	Medium
Formal Decision–Making Criteria	Medium	Medium	Medium	Medium
Shared Beliefs and Time	Low	Medium	Low	Medium
Informal Decision–Making Criteria	Medium	Medium	Low	Medium
Differentiation	High	Medium	Low	Low

N=95
Low means less than –.5 below the mean.
Medium means –.5 to .5 around the mean.
High means more than .5 above the mean.
See Appendix, particularly Table A.2, for the actual means and standard deviations.

Another reason this organization scored moderately, not low, on the decision-making authority dimension is that only certain decisions are important enough to require the attention of the entire staff and other, more mundane, decisions are handled by the executive director. This split is reflected in the three scenarios used to measure this dimension in the questionnaire.[2] All staff members made decisions concerning both the extended leave of absence request and the hiring decision. It was the executive director only who made the decision regarding the staff person who needed disciplining for making unauthorized long distance phone calls. The first two decisions are critical decisions; the third decision is a routine one. While my analysis lumps these three decisions together, future work would benefit from separating critical from noncritical decisions. Iannello's (1992) work on decision making in feminist organizations further substantiates the value of making such a distinction. What her work demonstrates (and my example glosses over) is that such a distinction is organizationally specific. Critical decisions for one organization may be considered quite routine in another. Thus, the goal would be to distinguish between the two within a particular empirical context, not to universally make claims about what kinds of decisions are critical and noncritical.

Professional Organizations

Twenty-six of the ninety-five organizations (twenty-seven percent) are best characterized as "professional organizations." This is the first of the hybrid forms that have a particular configuration of both bureaucratic and collectivist characteristics. Before describing this cluster, I want to make a point of clarification. As the discussion of the sampling procedure in the Appendix explains, one of the ways in which I defined the parameters of the study was to focus on organizations that produce "public goods" as opposed to "private goods." Because professional interest organizations (for example, Society of Women Engineers, Association of Real Estate Women) produce outcomes that are primarily consumed by the groups' members, I excluded these from the population. What this cluster represents, then, is a professional organization of a different kind. Namely, these are public goods-oriented nonprofits (of various types) that are dominated by professionals (for example, health care professionals, legal professionals, party politicians, mental health professionals).

There is some support for the idea of professions being a distinct organizational form (Hall 1968; Litwak 1961; Russell 1985). Likewise, my data show that organizations that are composed primarily of professional workers take on a distinct organizational form. What exactly do they look like?

Referring to Table 3.3, these groups are moderately differentiated in terms of division of labor, the members of the organization share similar political beliefs and spend some amount of time together beyond the work setting. Decision-making authority rests with the members of the organizations as a whole, however; and the group uses both formal and informal decision-making criteria in arriving at a decision. These organizations score low on both material incentives and normative incentives, which suggests the motivation for organizational participation may lie in the shared culture (that is, similar political beliefs and shared time outside work).

"City Rape Crisis" epitomizes a professional organization. Founded in 1984, this group is a rape crisis center in a large metropolitan hospital. The organization provides crisis intervention counseling to rape survivors in four emergency rooms in New York City. It conducts community outreach to educate the public about sexual assault, and it offers long-term individual and group counseling to sexual-assault survivors. Two-thirds of their funding comes from state and local government; the remaining one-third is made up in grants from private foundations.

City Rape Crisis is moderately differentiated (relative to this particular population of organizations) in terms of number of job positions and in terms of educational and economic background of organizational members. The paid staff consists of a director, assistant director, secretary, consultant who supervises counselors, and a part-time psychiatrist. The medical director of the hospital, the director of pediatrics and a steering committee of hospital professionals provide guidance and oversight. There are roughly 150 volunteers who serve in the capacity of crisis advocates, counselors, and interns. The assistant director describes the diversity among volunteers in the following manner:

> We have volunteers from all walks of life. The three women who come in twice a week to do volunteer work are all women in their 60s who don't have jobs and this is a place for them to come and help out. Another volunteer I'm thinking about has good computer skills; she's a housewife. Another volunteer who comes in teaches

special education and has some extra time... Another volunteer that comes and oversees the medical charts is a full-time nurse here... Then we might get a medical student who was originally working in the program for elective credit but continued on with us as a volunteer. (City Rape Crisis, November 7, 1991)

Additionally, despite this diversity in backgrounds and job positions, the majority of those who are connected to City Rape Crisis share similar views and spend time together outside the organization. This can be explained primarily by the fact that the participants are members of, or are closely associated with, the health profession. From the medical director of the hospital to the psychiatrist, to the counselors, to the nurse volunteer, to the medical student intern, these individuals share similar orientations and experiences because of their connection to the medical profession.

A third attribute of a professional organization is that decision-making authority rests with the group as a whole. Unlike collectivist organizations where this attribute is operationalized literally (each member of the collective has a say in all decisions), professional organizations realize collective decision-making authority more figuratively, namely through the internalization of collegial norms that takes place within a profession. So, in a particular situation, the paid staff may come up with a new policy idea, run it by the steering committee for input, and then formally implement it. Although the medical director and all the volunteers are not directly consulted, the decision is guided by the norms shared by the entire organization. The assistant director of City Rape Crisis describes how decisions are made in their organization:

The director ultimately makes the decisions. However, there are people she confers with, like the medical director, possibly our funders, our steering committee... We have a steering committee that's made up of different professionals who volunteer for the program; ...we'll confer with them as well. We're under the jurisdiction of the pediatrics department and there's an administrator of pediatrics, so she approves a lot before we go ahead as well. (City Rape Crisis, November 7, 1991)

Finally, professional organizations score low on material incentives and formal structures and low on normative incentives. Two points are important here. First, City Rape Crisis does not have formal structures (for example, disciplinary procedures, grievance procedures) for controlling behavior that are separate from those set forth in professional standards and codes of ethics. Likewise, policy and procedure manuals are few and vague, as the majority of technical actions are guided by hospital protocol. So, it is not that these structures do not exist; they simply are profession-generated rather than internal to the organization. Second, material incentives (for example, salary, benefits) and normative incentives (for example, personal empowerment, friendships with coworkers) are less meaningful in organizational settings full of professionals. What motivates members of City Rape Crisis is their commitment to the health profession itself and its values (that is, shared beliefs and time) rather than the specific material and normative incentives captured in the original framework.[3]

Pragmatic Collectives

The most populated of the four clusters is the second of the two hybrid forms. Forty-three of the organizations (forty-five percent) I call "pragmatic collectives." Like professional organizations, they combine aspects of both bureaucracy and collectives; however, the specific pattern of those components is distinct (see Table 3.3). Pragmatic collectives are similar to collectives in that they score low on differentiation and medium on decision-making authority. In other words, there are few distinctions made among job positions, and decision-making rests with a combination of groups and individuals. Pragmatic collectives are like bureaucracies in that they score low on normative incentives, low on shared beliefs and time, and moderate on formal decision-making criteria.

I selected the term "pragmatic *collectives*" because the core elements of collectives remain intact: low differentiation and collective decision-making authority (although an adulterated version). They are *pragmatic* collectives in that the collectivist elements that are compromised are related to practical concerns. For example, most of the women in these organizations are trying to make a living; thus, material incentives take priority over normative ones. Shared beliefs take a back seat, given the goal of many women's organizations to increase the racial and class diversity of their members. Time spent together outside the workplace is often unrealistic, given the numerous obligations placed on women in the 1980s-1990s. Formal decision-making criteria are used to help expedite otherwise time-consuming group decision-making processes.

"A Space of Her Own" represents a pragmatic collective. Founded in 1974, this organization is a unit within, and is housed on the campus of, a public university. The university is known as a "commuter campus" and serves a racially and ethnically diverse student body. The center itself caters to the women on campus, offering specific programs, providing information and referrals, and educating the college community about women's issues. While the center receives some financial support from the university, the majority of its sustenance comes from federal money and foundation grants. There are two full-time staff members (a director and an office manager) and between 11 and 25 part-time staff who come and go with outside grants.

A Space of Her Own is a pragmatic collective in the following ways. First, decisions are made at times by the director herself and at other times in conjunction with other members of the group, including the advisory board. The director of the center views this combination of individual authority and group authority this way:

> Everyone who works at the center has the freedom to shape the program how they wish. They consult me and it's rare I turn them down. So they have tremendous autonomy. In a way, I give them the same freedom that I have myself to shape their respective programs. . . .But, it makes sense to me that no one person should assume total control over an institution as complex as this. So, the first thing that I did is set up an advisory board and bring in people from different segments of the college community. . . .to provide oversight. Almost every project that I set up, I set up an advisory board to bring in new ideas and independent thoughts that help shape the program. (A Space of Her Own, October 9, 1990)

Second, actors (be they individuals or groups of individuals) rely primarily on formal criteria when making decisions. This is different from the "pure" collective and is justified in terms of speeding up the often time-consuming process of reaching decisions among a group of people. Third, material incentives, such as salary and opportunities for promotion, are valued in this organization far more than normative incentives, such as friendships with coworkers and opportunities to effect social change.

Fourth, sharing beliefs and spending social time with members of the organization are downplayed. Regarding shared beliefs, the director indicated that the only thing the members of the center share is the fact that they are women; they do not necessarily share similar politics or orientations:

> I never think that anybody comes [here] because they might have a feminist thought in their head. The program addresses personal, professional, and academic needs that they feel they have at a particular point in their lives… They may exit a feminist, but they certainly don't come in as such and the programs are not presented to them as such. They just happen to be for women. (A Space of Her Own, October 9, 1990)

The director had this to say about socializing with one another:

> [Our office manager] has always said over the years, "I wish more people hung out here." I've always said, "this is a place of work not a place for socializing." [However], students are welcome and encouraged to come in and sit down and use the library. They can have their lunch here, but it's just not a hangout. That's what I always thought—that this would be an administratively run center. It would be an office; it would mirror other academic offices, except that there would still be the opportunity for groups of students to use it. (A Space of Her Own, October 9, 1990)

According to the director, A Space of Her Own was not always structured the way it was at the time of my contact with them in 1990. From 1974 to 1980, the center was marginally positioned in the college community, the members had an explicit radical feminist ideology, the focus was on supporting the college women through peer counseling, and it ran more like a "pure" collective. When the political climate changed in the early 1980s, the center went through a crisis. Because there was no longer support for their radical feminist ideology or services on campus, they turned to the outside community for purpose. Providing counseling services for community women became the main focus, further marginalizing the center on campus. The current director was hired in 1985 to revitalize the center. A key part of the revitalization was to make changes in the center's structure by introducing more formality and broadening their conception of feminism.

It is uncertain whether the center's structural development will stop here with the hybrid form or move toward a more traditional, bureaucratic form. I should also note that the center's development from a collective to a pragmatic collective is not unusual among the other pragmatic collectives in this study, but it is by no means a requisite path. Furthermore, not all of the hybrids of this type are units within parent organizations as is A Space of Her Own.

Looking at the women's nonprofit sector in New York City, we can describe the variation in organizational form in terms of four types: bureaucracies, professional organizations, pragmatic collectives and collectives. Discovering bureaucracies, hybrids, and collectives is not news. But discovering that nearly two-thirds of women's nonprofits in this locale are *hybrids*, being able to specify *types* of hybrids, and specifying their exact *configuration* is news. Now, what explains this variation in form and why does it matter? I turn to these questions in the next chapter.

4

WHY DO WOMEN'S NONPROFITS
LOOK THE WAY THEY DO?

There is a fair amount of theory in both organizational sociology and in the social movements literature that concerns itself with predicting and explaining organizational structure, style or form. The literature is limited, however, in that the focus is on ideal typical forms of organization at the two extreme ends of the organizational structure continuum, particularly bureaucracy and collectives. Therefore, we have theory that predicts bureaucratic structures over collective styles of organizations and vice versa. Although existing theory certainly anticipates the existence of hybrid forms of organizational structure, we have little theoretical insight as to what explains (or predicts) hybrid forms. Because the majority of the nonprofit women's organizations in this study are hybrids, this lack of theory is particularly problematic.

The first part of this chapter concerns itself strictly with the two end points of the organizational structure continuum in their ideal typical form. First, what does organizational and social movement theory identify as predictors of bureaucratic and collectivist structures? And second, based on bivariate analysis of these predictors and organizational form, how do these theoretical ideas stand up to the empirical case of women's nonprofits in contemporary New York City?

The second part of the chapter asks whether the same predictors that have been proposed by theorists to understand bureaucratic and collectivist structures have any utility when it comes to hybrid forms. I will argue that they offer little, if any, insight into hybrid forms of organization. Because of this, I turn my attention to the qualitative interviews with women who work in hybrid organizations, and I offer some preliminary explanation as to why these women have adopted the hybrid organizational form.

Predicting Bureaucracies and Collectives: Theoretical Explanations

Both social movement theory and organizational theory are relevant to a discussion about organizational structure or form.

Social Movement Theory

Social movement scholars have long explored the question of why social movements take a particular form. Overwhelmingly, they explain a social movement's structure by looking at the prevailing ideology of the leadership and/or membership. As the ideology changes so, too, does the movement's form. A classic example is Michels' (1962) claims about the German Social Democratic Party. Initially, the party was internally democratic to match its socialist principles. As the party moved to attain more political power, members were "seduced into abandoning their principles" (Rothschild & Whitt, 1986), and internal democracy was replaced by oligarchy, or rule by a small group of elite members. The inevitability of oligarchization has been applied beyond Michels' original case to social movements in general.

In the context of the women's movement, the connection between ideology and organizational structure has been made explicit historically (Ferree & Hess, 1994; Freeman, 1974). As discussed in Chapter 1, for the most part the younger strand of the women's movement was characterized by a radical feminist ideology (including radical, anarchist, socialist, Marxist feminist) and a strong desire to set up groups and organizations using collectivist principles. The older strand of the women's movement adopted a more liberal feminist ideology and used conventionally structured, bureaucratic organizations to their advantage.

While the focus on ideology makes theoretical sense from a social movement standpoint and is empirically valid in explaining social movement structure in certain circumstances, it does not capture all we know about *organizational* structure. That is, social movements are made up of organizations, so any explanation should be as much about organizational structure as it is about social movement behavior.

Two traditions in complex organizational theory are helpful in explaining why an organization takes on a particular form: neo-institutional theory and contingency theory. Both theories were developed with large organizations in mind, and the majority of organizations in my study are small. Since both theories are presented as *general* theories of organizations, however, their key elements should apply here. If not, they need to be qualified. Let's review the elements of the theories.

Neo-institutional Theory

Neo-institutional theory emphasizes the constraints an institutional environment places on organizations, as well as the effects organizations as institutions have on their surroundings. The external environment and other organizations are important considerations for understanding what form an organization takes.

Adopting a neo-institutional perspective, Zucker (1983) documents historically the institutionalization of the rational, bureaucratic organizational form. Institutionalization is defined as "the process through which components of formal structure become widely accepted, as both appropriate and necessary, and serve to legitimate organizations" (Zucker 1983:25). This "organization as institution" approach suggests that the structure of bureaucratic organization itself, and its underlying assumptions and values, become taken-for-granted. This phenomenological process of taken-for-grantedness renders the possibility of alternative modes of organization virtually unthinkable. According to Zucker, the bureaucratic organization, once institutionalized in the 1920s, powerfully shaped its environment, including other forms of organization, group life, and social movement activity. Therefore, very few groups come together without adopting structures of formal, bureaucratic organization, even if they are antithetical to the group's work or ideology. When individuals forming organizations do explicitly challenge institutionalized definitions of "appropriate" form (for example, through political struggle), they are not necessarily immune from all institutional pressure. Groups may be aware of alternative styles of organization and plan to adopt such alternative structures, but find that in order to achieve their goals (or simply survive) they must conform to standards set by their institutional environment. DiMaggio and Powell (1983:150) describe this process as coercive isomorphism, where pressure is "exerted on organizations by other organizations upon which they are dependent and by cultural expectations in the society within which organizations function." DiMaggio and Powell find support for this process in the literature on collectivist organizations in general. Citing the findings of Milofsky (1981) and Swidler (1979), they suggest that alternative organizations may take on more conventional structures in order to receive funding from, or interact with, a hierarchical bureaucratic organization. Therefore, the relationship between ideology and structure is compromised.

To understand the structure of a particular women's organization, then, we need to describe the institutional environment of that particular organization, see how the environment is structured, and show how the environment interfaces with the focal organization.

The case of Radical Women (RW), a socialist-feminist political action organization, illustrates the influence the environment has on an organization's structure. Martin (1986:125-126), one of the founders of the group, documents how the Freedom Socialist Party (FSP) affected Radical Women both programmatically and structurally. Although formed as an autonomous women's collective in 1967, it became an official affiliate of FSP in the early 1970s. Martin attributes the survival of Radical Women to its link with FSP. At a time when many feminist organizations were dissolving, RW relied on the well-established foundation of FSP's theory and practice. The tight link to FSP is responsible for the specific form RW adopted: democratic centralism, a form characteristic of the male-dominated new left. Democratic centralism is a step away from participatory collectivism in that policy decisions are made through a majority voting system rather than through consensus among all members (Martin 1986; Radical Women 1973).

Contingency Theory

Contingency theory focuses on the internal dynamics of organizations. The internal tasks (that is, technology or work performed) are the primary determinants of organizational structure. If tasks are routine, then formal, centralized structures are indicated; if technology is nonroutine or unpredictable, then flexible "organismic" structures are more appropriate (Burns 1971; Perrow 1967; Perrow 1986).

This distinction in tasks is exemplified by the different work performed within the National Organization for Women (NOW). While NOW is a single organization with unitary goals, the work performed in the local chapters differs considerably from the tasks carried out at the national headquarters. In the early years of the organization's existence, the executive body of NOW was primarily engaged in sex-discrimination litigation. In contrast, the local chapters were preoccupied with networking, demonstrating, and forming study groups (Carden 1974; Ferree & Hess 1994). The former tasks were more conducive to conventional, bureaucratic structures. Thus, the national headquarters was composed of an executive board of officers, written charter, and a formal decision process. At the local level, NOW chapters were alternatively organized, often participatory and egalitarian in structure (Carden 1974:112). While this example is intended to illustrate the connection between technology and structure, it also introduces the idea that bureaucracies can have diverse subunits. These subunits may be protected by the larger bureaucracy from any outside pressure, as this case illustrates. Or, the subunits may be subjected to external environmental pressure of their own as neo-institutional theory predicts.

Other Organizational Predictors of Form

Besides environment and tasks, two other factors in the complex organizational literature are potential predictors of organizational form: size and age. What do we know about size and age? In a review of eighty empirical studies of size and organizational structure, which were published between 1950 and 1974, Kimberly (1976) argues that size has been conceptualized and defined too globally and inconsistently for us to be able to say anything definitive about its relationship to structure. Size has been measured in diverse ways: number of employees, capacity, number of clients, net assets, and sales volume. This concept has been employed as both a structural characteristic and as a constraint on structure. Size also has been used as a cause of structure and as an effect of structure. Despite the state of the scholarship on size, we can say at least two things: a) bureaucracy is characteristic of large organizations (Blau 1970; Weber 1978); and b) collectivist structures are most likely to succeed in small organizations (Michels 1962; Rothschild & Whitt 1986).

For the relationship between organizational age and structure, there are two competing ideas in the organizational literature. First, Stinchcombe (1965:143) claims that there is a "correlation between the time in history that a particular type of organization was invented and the social structure of organizations of that type which exist at the present time." Put another way, organizations that are born during the same era will look alike and will carry that structural "imprint" for the duration of their lives.

In contrast, the organizational life cycle literature claims that an organization looks and acts a particular way depending on which stage of its life cycle it is in. One formulation of this perspective suggests that as an organization ages, it inevitably progresses through five stages of development (Perkins, Nieva, & Lawler 1983). The initial stage of this cycle has characteristics similar to the collectives described here. Later stages take on characteristics of bureaucracy. What is problematic about this perspective is the assumption that collectivism is never an end, in and of itself.

In summary, social movement theory and complex organization theory are potentially useful for understanding why organizations adopt certain structures. An organization's ideology, technology, environment, size and age are competing factors in determining organizational form. Figure 4.1 illustrates the relationships among these competing factors. In the next section, I operationalize the key theoretical concepts—ideology, tasks, and environment, size, age— and then test their relationship to organizational form using a series of bivariate cross tabulations.

Operationalization of Key Concepts

Ideology, tasks, environment, size, and age were the core independent variables in the initial stage of statistical analysis.

FIGURE 4.1
Predictors of Organizational Form

General Relationships:

Ideology -- >	
Task --- >	
Environment --- >	Organizational
Size -- >	Form
Age --- >	

Specific Relationships:

Non-feminist or liberal feminist ideology ----------------------------- >	bureaucracy
Radical feminist ideology --- >	collective
Routine tasks -- >	bureaucracy
Nonroutine tasks -- >	collective
Government funding, traditional environment ----------------------- >	bureaucracy
No government funding, alternative environment ------------------- >	collective
Large paid staff -- >	bureaucracy
Small or no paid staff -- >	collective
Older organization- --- >	bureaucracy (life cycle perspective) collective (imprint perspective)
Younger organization --- >	collective (life cycle perspective) bureaucracy (imprint perspective)

Ideology

Ideology was operationalized as whether a women's group considers itself a feminist organization (either in membership or purpose). The meaning of "feminist" was purposefully left undefined to allow for the greatest breadth of interpretation. Those organizations that did self-identify as feminist were asked to specify the meaning of feminism and to further identify their particular brand of feminism (conservative, liberal, radical, anarchist, socialist, Marxist, other). As I have already suggested, organizations with radical feminist ideology (including radical, anarchist, socialist, Marxist) will be associated with collectivist structures; organizations with conservative, liberal or no feminist ideology will be more traditionally structured.

Unfortunately, I cannot make fine-grained distinctions in feminist ideology with this group of organizations. Over half (twenty-nine) of the explicitly *feminist* organizations (n=52) claimed in the questionnaire that they do not further specify, or label, their ideology. During a subsequent interview, one woman responded as follows:

> In a sense, it's a silent awareness of everyone who participates that, yes, we really do subscribe to feminism. And, we're here because of it. But, we don't promote one [feminism] or another. . .So, I think in terms of the best of what's being said at the moment in terms of feminist theory, we would be right there, from what I know. But any one theory or another, any one philosophy or another, no. (Education 1, August 1, 1990)

This finding is consistent with the claim made by Ferree and Hess (1994) that when the women's movement finds itself reacting to a hostile political environment, as it did in the 1980s, movement members pull together, internal ideological conflicts decline and, therefore, differences among varieties of feminisms become less significant.

As in the above quote, most people did not elaborate on the reasons why their organizations do not further specify their feminist ideology. There were, however, some exceptions. One woman expressed frustration with the conventional categories of feminism (for example, liberal, radical, socialist, Marxist) by scrawling in red ink in the margins of the questionnaire: "Geez! Why not get away from such simplistic categorizations?" (General 12). During an interview, another pointed out that such categories were no longer meaningful distinctions to make: "Radical is not necessarily an appropriate term anymore. It's beside the point whether an [organization] is radical or not" (General 10, March 13, 1992). According to another interviewee, a group that is obsessive about specifying its brand of feminism

> …keeps the organization very limited from grassroots women— from normal women in the community. I also think that it acts as a barrier to people who don't have any formal education. The political discussions, unless you're really interested in politics, most people don't feel that affects their lives. (Rape 1, October 9, 1991)

In addition, given the political climate in the late 1980s, it was "radical" enough for organizations to use the term feminist to describe their ideology; specifying additional labels that implied more extreme positions within feminism was viewed as too risky. Two women from different organizations put it this way:

> I think feminists have a bad name. The word (I love the word) has a wonderful history and I think it's really rich, but I know a lot of people for whom it sticks in their craw. They don't know what it means, really. They don't have any historical context. They think it sounds more radical than really who they are. (Health Education 2, October 25, 1991)

> I made a conscious decision not to be ideological about the feminism that identifies with [the organization]. In fact, I think we have to be very cautious about using the "F" word. . .A woman I feel I know real well kiddingly said the first time we exchanged ideas on our programs at a conference, "You know what I call our feminism? I call it Tupperware feminism." She's very much identified in radical lesbian circles in her community and she moved into this job and turned on a very different public image. Her philosophy is not in any way compromised; she's just couching it all differently. (University Center 6, October 9, 1990)

Only nine organizations adopted a label more radical than "liberal feminist." For this analysis, then, the distinction in ideology will be between "feminist" and "non-feminist" organizations. We would expect that organizations with a feminist ideology should be collectivist or bureaucratic in structure (because we are grouping together radical and liberal feminists); groups without a feminist ideology should be bureaucratically structured.

Tasks

Organizational task (technology; work) was operationalized following Perrow's (1967) distinction between routine and nonroutine work. Routine tasks involve few exceptional cases and, when exceptions do occur, they are easily analyzable. Conversely, tasks are nonroutine if many exceptional cases are encountered and few analytic techniques exist for analyzing these situations.

Questionnaire respondents were asked to think about the three major tasks carried out in their organization and indicate the extent of their agreement or disagreement with the following kinds of statements:

a) Frequently, questions, problems or exceptions arise while doing our major activities (to measure exceptional cases).
b) When a question, problem, or exception comes up there is usually an easy solution (to measure analyzability).

Three measures of exceptional cases and three measures of analyzability were then combined into one aggregate score of routineness. Routine tasks are associated with bureaucracy; nonroutine tasks are associated with collectivist forms.

Environment

An organization's environment was operationalized in relationship to funding and inter-organizational interactions. First, respondents were asked about their organization's sources of funding. For this portion of the analysis, I was interested in whether an organization receives government funding. Although neo-institutional theory predicts that government funding would lead an organization to adopt a bureaucratic form, previous research on women's organizations is mixed in terms of the impact of government funding on organizational structure. Some suggest government funding requires organizations to adopt bureaucratic structures (Johnson 1981; Sullivan 1982). Others question the inevitability of the impact, leaving open the possibility that women's organizations can resist bureaucratic pressure or even affect government structures and practices themselves (Matthews 1994; Martin 1990; Reinelt 1994). Therefore, I am interested in determining here whether there is a relationship between type of funding and organizational form.

Funding, however, is not the only environmental factor influencing an organization. Respondents were also asked to characterize the extent of their interactions with *all* external organizations and institutions (for example, businesses, government agencies, religious groups, political parties, social service agencies, ethnic groups, community action groups, unions, local feminist groups, feminist groups outside New York City). Here, environment was conceptualized in line with DiMaggio and Powell's definition of organizational field. The environment refers to all the organizations that "constitute a recognized area of institutional life: key suppliers, resources and product consumers, regulatory agencies, and other organizations that produce similar services or products" (DiMaggio & Powell 1983:148).

Based on this conceptualization, an organization's environment was classified as being feminist or traditional. A feminist environment means the majority of an executive director's (or equivalent) contact with the outside organizational world (including telephone conversations, communication by mail, or personal contacts) is with feminist or woman-centered groups. A traditional environment means the director's contact with the outside organizational world is primarily with traditional groups (that is, government agencies, businesses, social service agencies, ethnic/cultural groups, churches or synagogues, political parties, community action groups). Organizations living in a conventional environment are more likely to be bureaucratic in structure; organizations living in a feminist environment will have a greater opportunity to be alternatively structured.

Size

Size was defined by the number of full-time staff (both paid and volunteer) who work for the organization. I then classified the organizations into two categories: small (zero to ten full-time workers) and large (eleven or more full-timers). It is important to stress that my use of the terms small and large is relative. Compared with the range of organizational sizes in the world at large, the majority of the organizations in this population are relatively small. Nonetheless, following previous organizational research, we should expect bigger organizations to be more bureaucratic than smaller ones. Conversely, smaller organizations are more likely to be collectivist in structure.

Age

Age was determined by the year in which the organization was started. Organizations founded between 1967 and 1979 constituted the older group of organizations. Organizations that were born between 1980 and 1988 were considered the younger organizations. If Stinchcombe (1965) is correct, the older organizations should be collectivist in structure because they were imprinted as such during the early years of the women's movement. Younger organizations should be more bureaucratic. In contrast, if the life cycle perspective is correct, the older organizations should be more bureaucratic and the younger organizations more collectivist.

The Results

To test the relationship between the five core independent variables (ideology, task, environment, size, and age) and the dependent variable (organizational form), I conducted bivariate cross tabulations, which are displayed in Tables 4.1 through 4.7. I should note that because I am working with the *population* of women's nonprofits in New York City, not a *sample* of organizations, I am concerned with substantive rather statistical significance. Below, I discuss the results in order of the importance of the findings.

Age

Age is, by far, the strongest predictor of organizational form. As Table 4.1 indicates, older organizations are much more likely to be structured bureaucratically than collectively. Conversely, younger organizations are more likely to be collectives than bureaucracies. This is consistent with the life cycle perspective on organizational age discussed above. The mean date of foundation for the bureaucracies is 1976 and the mean date of foundation for collectives is 1981.

TABLE 4.1
Date of Foundation
by Organizational Form

Date of Foundation	Organizational Form		
	Bureaucracy	Collective	Total
Older	88%	12%	100%
1967-1979	(15)	(2)	(17)
Younger	38%	62%	100%
1980-1988	(3)	(5)	(8)

N=25
missing=1

Ideology

Ideology is also helpful in predicting organizational form. As Table 4.2 shows, organizations without a feminist ideology are equally as likely to be bureaucratic or collectivist in structure. However, organizations with a feminist ideology are much more likely to adopt bureaucratic structures over collectivist ones. If we assume that not all of the feminist organizations are liberal feminist in ideology, this finding is contrary to the theoretical expectations discussed earlier.

Once we disaggregate the feminist category into strands of feminism we see that, in fact, not all are liberal feminist organizations (see Table 4.3). Organizations that have an unspecified feminist ideology are more than twice as likely to be bureaucratic as collectivist. All of the liberal feminist organizations are bureaucratic. And, contrary to our predictions, the one radical feminist organization is also bureaucratic.

TABLE 4.2
Ideology by Organizational Form

Ideology	Organizational Form		
	Bureaucracy	Collective	Total
Not feminist	50%	50%	100%
	(5)	(5)	(10)
Feminist	81%	19%	100%
	(13)	(3)	(16)

N=26
missing=0
NOTE: *Not feminist* includes the following: groups that do not consider themselves feminist organizations either in membership or purpose; groups that have not resolved whether they consider themselves feminist organizations either in membership or purpose; groups where the subject of feminism has never come up. *Feminist* means the group considers itself a feminist organization either in membership or purpose.

TABLE 4.3
Ideology by Organizational Form
Disaggregating Feminist Ideology

Ideology	Organizational Form		
	Bureaucracy	Collective	Total
Not feminist	50%	50%	100%
	(5)	(5)	(10)
Feminist (unspecified)	70%	30%	100%
	(7)	(3)	(10)
Feminist (liberal)	100%	0%	100%
	(5)	(0)	(5)
Feminist (radical)	100%	0%	100%
	(1)	(0)	(1)

N=26
missing=0
NOTE: *Not feminist* includes the following: groups that do not consider themselves feminist organizations either in membership or purpose; groups that have not resolved whether they consider themselves feminist organizations either in membership or purpose; groups where the subject of feminism has never come up. *Feminist* means the group considers itself a feminist organization either in membership or purpose.

Tasks

As for the relationship between tasks and organizational form, the findings are partially consistent with contingency theory (see Table 4.4). Organizations with routine tasks are more likely to adopt bureaucratic structures than collectivist ones. Organizations with nonroutine tasks, however, are equally as likely to be bureaucratic or collectivist in form. How might we explain this latter finding, which goes against theoretical predictions?

First, like other studies in the contingency theory tradition, this study has not made a distinction between technical work and other kinds of work that are carried out in an organization. My interview data reveal at least four different types of work that may or may not coincide with technical work on level of routineness. Besides technical work, organizations in this sample engage in political work (lobbying, testifying, advocacy), educational work (disseminating information), and economic work (securing funds for the operation of the organization). These categories are not mutually exclusive. For example, an organization's technical work can be educational work. The point is, my measures of routineness on the questionnaire are measures of routineness on "work" generically, without distinguishing between technical, political, educational, and economic.

Second, measures of routineness obtained in the questionnaires were completed by the executive director (or equivalent) of each organization. It seems plausible that I might have asked the wrong person to judge routineness of work. Often times, line staff workers and volunteers do the bulk of the technical work in these groups; executive directors are more likely involved in political, educational, or economic work. Therefore, the executive directors were asked to judge work that they may not have been engaged in directly.

Finally, there is always the possibility that there is something about work other than routineness or nonroutineness that is more important for predicting organizational structure. All three of these possibilities may explain the results I obtained in Table 4.4. In addition, they have implications for other studies that have been carried out in the contingency theory tradition.

TABLE 4.4
Task by Organizational Form

Tasks	Organizational Form		
	Bureaucracy	Collective	Total
Routine	82%	18%	100%
	(9)	(2)	(11)
Non-routine	54%	46%	100%
	(7)	(6)	13

N=24
missing=2
NOTE: *Routine* tasks are those that involve few exceptional cases and, when exceptions
do occur, they are easy to analyze. *Nonroutine* tasks are those that involve many
exceptional cases where few techniques exist for analyzing them.

Environment

The remaining three independent variables (environment,
government funding, size) are less useful than the others in predicting
organizational structure. Tables 4.5 and 4.6 exhibit the relationship
between environment and organizational form. First, as displayed in

TABLE 4.5
Environment by Organizational Form

Environment	Organizational Form		
	Bureaucracy	Collective	Total
Feminist	88%	12%	100%
	(7)	(1)	(8)
Traditional	61%	39%	100%
	(11)	(7)	(18)

N=26
missing=0
NOTE: *Feminist* environment means the majority of an executive director's (or
equivalent) contact with the outside organizational world (including telephone
conversations, communication by mail, or personal contacts) is with feminist or woman-
centered groups. *Traditional* environment means the majority of an executive director's
(or equivalent) contact with the outside organizational world (including telephone
conversations, communication by mail, or personal contacts) is with traditional groups
(that is, government agencies, businesses, social service agencies, ethnic/cultural groups,
churches or synagogues, political parties, community action groups).

TABLE 4.6
Government Funding by Organizational Form

Government Funding	Organizational Form		
	Bureaucracy	Collective	Total
No	73%	27%	100%
	(8)	(3)	(11)
Yes	67%	33%	100%
	(10)	(5)	(15)

N=26
missing=0

NOTE: *No* government funding includes groups for which zero percent of their total support (including financial, as well as donations of goods and services) comes from the local, state, or federal government. *Yes* includes those organizations that receive any amount of support (including financial, as well as donations of goods and services) from the local, state, or federal government.

Table 4.5, regardless of whether organizations live in traditional environments or feminist environments, they are more likely to be bureaucracies than collectives. Second, regardless of whether organizations receive government funding, they are more likely to be bureaucratic than collective in form (Table 4.6).

Size

As Table 4.7 reveals, small organizations are twice as likely to be bureaucratic as collectivist. Similarly, large organizations are more likely to be bureaucratic than collectivist. I am unable to report the actual mean size for each of the organizational forms because organizations were asked to categorize their size (0-2; 3-5; 6-10; 11-25; 26-50; more than 50) as opposed to specifying exact numbers of full-time staff. I can say, however, that the bureaucracies are the largest, followed by collectives, professional organizations, and pragmatic collectives.

Predicting the Hybrid Organizational Forms

Do the same independent variables used to explain why organizations adopt bureaucratic versus collectivist structures help us

TABLE 4.7
Size of Staff
by Organizational Form

Size of Staff	Organizational Form		
	Bureaucracy	Collective	Total
Small	67%	33%	100%
0-10	(10)	(5)	(15)
Large	73%	27%	100%
11+	(8)	(3)	(11)

N=26
missing=0

NOTE: *Small* and *Large* refer to the number of people who work full-time for the organization, including officers, governing board members, staff, and volunteers.

in making predictions about the hybrid organizations that exist in this study (that is, the professional organizations and the pragmatic-collectives)? I repeated the bivariate analyses presented above using professional organizations and pragmatic collectives as the two categories of the dependent variable. The results are presented in Tables 4.8 through 4.14. With the exception of organizational size, the independent variables are not useful predictors of hybrid structures. This is not surprising given the fact that these variables were generated from theory that explicitly focused on predicting bureaucratic and collectivist styles of organization.

Table 4.8 displays the relationship between size and hybrid organizational form. It is clear from these results that small organizations are twice as likely to have a pragmatic-collectivist structure as a professional one. And, large organizations are twice as likely to have a professional structure as a pragmatic-collectivist structure. I will return to the issue of size in a moment. As Tables 4.9 through 4.14 reveal, regardless of the independent variable (ideology, environment, task, or age), organizations are more likely to be pragmatic-collectives than professional organizations.

If these standard variables (with the exception of size) do not provide insight into why organizations adopt hybrid structures, then what does? To answer this question, I returned to the interviews I conducted

TABLE 4.8
Size of Staff
by Hybrid Organizational Form

Size of Staff	Organizational Form		
	Professional	Pragmatic-Collective	Total
Small 0-10	33% (20)	67% (40)	100% (60)
Large 11+	67% (6)	33% (3)	100% (9)

N=69
missing=0
NOTE: *Small* and *Large* refer to the number of people who work full time for the organization, including officers, governing board members, staff, and volunteers.

with members of the hybrid organizations. The analysis of the qualitative data confirms the importance of size (with interesting nuance) and suggests two additional variables that help explain the existence of hybrid structures. All three are related, but discussed in turn below: size, organizational constituency, and networking as core work.

TABLE 4.9
Ideology by Hybrid Organizational Form

Ideology	Organizational Form		
	Professional	Pragmatic-Collective	Total
Not feminist	42% (14)	58% (19)	100% (33)
Feminist	33% (12)	67% (24)	100% (36)

N=69
missing=0
NOTE: *Not feminist* includes the following: groups that do not consider themselves feminist organizations either in membership or purpose; groups that have not resolved whether they consider themselves feminist organizations either in membership or purpose; groups where the subject of feminism has never come up. *Feminist* means the group considers itself a feminist organization either in membership or purpose.

TABLE 4.10
Ideology by Hybrid Organizational Form
Disaggregating Feminist Ideology

Ideology	Organizational Form		
	Professional	Pragmatic-Collective	Total
Not feminist	42% (14)	58% (19)	100% (33)
Feminist (unspecified)	32% (6)	68% (13)	100% (19)
Feminist (liberal)	44% (4)	56% (5)	100% (9)
Feminist (radical)	25% (2)	75% (6)	100% (8)

N=69
missing=0

NOTE: *Not feminist* includes the following: groups that do not consider themselves feminist organizations either in membership or purpose; groups that have not resolved whether they consider themselves feminist organizations either in membership or purpose; groups where the subject of feminism has never come up. *Feminist* means the group considers itself a feminist organization either in membership or purpose.

TABLE 4.11
Government Funding by Hybrid Organizational Form

Goverment Funding	Organizational Form		
	Professional	Pragmatic-Collective	Total
No	33% (12)	67% (24)	100% (36)
Yes	42% (14)	58% (19)	100% (33)

N=69
missing=0

NOTE: *No* government funding includes groups for which zero percent of their total support (including financial, as well as donations of goods and services) comes from the local, state, or federal government. *Yes* includes those organizations that receive any amount of support (including financial, as well as donations of goods and services) from the local, state, or federal government.

TABLE 4.12
Environment by Hybrid Organizational Form

Environment	Organizational Form		
	Professional	Pragmatic-Collective	Total
Feminist	38% (5)	62% (8)	100% (13)
Traditional	35% (19)	65% (35)	100% (54)

N=67
missing=2

NOTE: *Feminist* environment means the majority of an executive director's (or equivalent) contact with the outside organizational world (including telephone conversations, communication by mail, or personal contacts) is with feminist or woman-centered groups. *Traditional* environment means the majority of an executive director's (or equivalent) contact with the outside organizational world (including telephone conversations, communication by mail, or personal contacts) is with traditional groups (that is, government agencies, businesses, social service agencies, ethnic/cultural groups, churches or synagogues, political parties, community action groups).

TABLE 4.13
Task by Hybrid Organizational Form

Tasks	Organizational Form		
	Professional	Pragmatic-Collective	Total
Routine	34% (11)	66% (21)	100% (32)
Non-routine	40% (14)	60% (21)	100% (35)

N=67
missing=2

NOTE: *Routine* tasks are those that involve few exceptional cases and, when exceptions do occur, they are easy to analyze. *Nonroutine* tasks are those that involve many exceptional cases where few techniques exist for analyzing them.

TABLE 4.14
Date of Foundation
by Hybrid Organizational Form

Date of Foundation	Organizational Form		
	Professional	Pragmatic-Collective	Total
Older 1967-1979	39% (15)	61% (23)	100% (38)
Younger 1980-1988	34% (10)	66% (19)	100% (29)

N=67
missing=2

Size

Returning to previous discussions about size, for this population of organizations, bureaucratically structured groups are the largest organizations, followed closely by collectives. Professional organizations are smaller than both, but larger than pragmatic-collectives. Because the bureaucracies and collectives are so close in size, it is understandable that size would not be a meaningful predictor of organizational form for those cases, but a meaningful one for the latter two categories. In addition, what the qualitative analysis reveals is the importance of the extreme smallness of pragmatic collectives. It is the extreme nature of their size that helps make sense out of why they look the way they do (that is, why they adopt structures that combine some of the qualities of collectives with some of the structural characteristics that typify bureaucracy) and why members of these organizations talk about structure (or more accurately, don't talk about it) in the way that they do.

As Chapter 3 showed, there are two major factors that distinguish pragmatic-collectives from the other forms. First, they are collective-like in that they have little differentiation among members and adopt a version of collective decision-making. What their extreme smallness suggests, and the interviews confirm, however, is they do this not out of some commitment to collectivist ideals, but because of their size. How differentiated can an organization be with one or two staff members? How possible is it to not make decisions among yourselves when there are only two of you working in the organization?

Second, these organizations are bureaucratic-like (I term this pragmatic) in that they score low on normative incentives, low on shared beliefs and time, and moderate on formal decision-making criteria. Again, I'd like to suggest that these are a function of their small size. With few staff members, it seems likely that the focus would be on survival (both organizational and individual) rather than abstract concerns. If there is only one paid staff member who must also work a part-time job to pay her rent, that necessity threatens the very existence of the organization. With few staff members, it is conceivable that a concerted effort would be made to maximize the diversity among staff rather than have two like-minded and similarly skilled people. With few staff, it makes sense that there would be little or no need for formal criteria to guide decision-making.

In interviews, the women who work in pragmatic-collectives were often confused and frustrated with my questions about organizational structure. Unlike the early days of the women's movement, they didn't engage in philosophical or concrete discussions about structural models. Such discussions didn't make any sense because of their size. In the absence of any commitment (philosophically or otherwise) to a particular organizational form, survival (the pragmatics of getting the work done) generates organizational form. The co-director of one educational organization did not even think of her organization as having any structure:

> What do you mean, structure? We have no formal structure. We're like an amoeba. We have a job to do and we just do it—whatever it takes. Everyone does everything all at once. I guess you could say we just happen. (Education 3, March 5, 1992)

The director of A Space of Her Own was equally frustrated by my queries about organizational structure:

> I don't see that there's enough of us to even talk about structure. I'm the only full-time person, so who would these other people be

to involve in decisions or delegate responsibility?… That's why I have to go outside the center. For every project that I set up, I set up an advisory board and bring in people from different segments of the community who have new ideas, independent thoughts and work to help shape the program. (A Space of Her Own, October 9, 1990)

In both these cases, the structure emerges from the process of doing the work of the organization. This leads to the second factor that helps explain hybrid organizational forms—both pragmatic-collectives and professional organizations: the organizational constituency. Who is doing the work and who the work is for is another piece to the hybrid puzzle.

Organizational Constituency

I am using the term organizational constituency in two ways: those who work for the organization and those served by the organization. Professional organizations, by definition, are made up primarily of professional workers of some sort (for example, health care professionals, legal professionals, mental health professionals). Although professionals may work in bureaucracies, collectives, and pragmatic-collectives, when they dominate the workforce of an organization, they influence the very structure of that organization. Thus, in a very straightforward way, a professional worker constituency is a predictor of the professional organizational form.

Constituency is also a meaningful predictor of the pragmatic-collective organizational form. Instead of being dominated by professionals, however, pragmatic-collectives are dominated by minority groups and/or concentrate their efforts on serving minority populations. Minority groups include racial minorities, ethnic minorities, the disabled, lesbians and gay men, and the elderly. Fifty-one percent of pragmatic-collectives have a minority focus or constituency compared to only thirty-three percent of the entire population of women's nonprofits in New York City. Although minority groups may work in, or be served by, bureaucracies, collectives, and professional organizations, they are dominant in pragmatic-collectives.

This emphasis on minority populations is built into the very purpose of the organization, which is reflected in the organizations' statement of purpose. Here is a sample of this minority emphasis:

[Domestic Violence 4] provides direct services for Asian Pacific women who are confronting the problem of violence against women (domestic violence, rape). We provide public education to increase the public's understanding of violence and rape in the Asian community and to increase the community support to eliminate such problems.

[Employment 1] works to improve the economic status of working poor Black women.

[Rape 4] offers counseling, advocacy and general assistance to men and women who have experienced anti-gay/anti-lesbian violence, sexual assault, domestic violence and other forms of victimization.

[Education 3]'s mission is to promote equal educational opportunity through programs and material that counteract bias due to sex, race, disability, and low income. Our approach is inclusive— meaning that we pay attention to the connections between these long-standing and interrelated biases, which limit individual potential and have particularly adverse affect on women and children.

Networking As Core Work

Very much related to the extremely small size (and corresponding issues of survival) and minority constituency of pragmatic-collectives is what I call "networking as core work." This factor, I propose, distinguishes pragmatic-collectives not only from professional organizations, but from bureaucracies and collectives as well. Networking as core work is distinct from the activity of networking that all women's organizations are involved in to some degree. This concept suggests that the primary and core work that the organization is involved in is connecting and forming alliances with diverse constituencies outside the organization. This networking as core work takes primacy over and, in some cases, replaces other work, such as providing direct services, advocating for legal or social change, and educating the larger society on issues relevant to women's lives.

In some cases, networking becomes core work because of the larger mission of the organization. Health Education 4's entire purpose is to mobilize women around the issue of reproductive freedom. The organization works on establishing and then strengthening geographical network connections among women and on building coalitions with other organizations that support a pro-choice position. Given their mandate, the way they do their work (forming ties with others) is in actuality, *the* work. Likewise, the director of A Space of Her Own, writing in an article about her organization, connects networking to the group's overall mission.

> Networking is probably the cornerstone of our success. Our motto is that whatever programming we do, we do it together with others. In so doing we prove ourselves useful and fulfill our mission to create a community of concern around women's issues. (A Space of Her Own, Document B)

In other cases, networking becomes core work because without ties to the external world, the small organization would not survive. When Rape 10 lost funding from one of its major grantors, full-time staff was cut by more than half, necessitating moving outside the organization for support. This new networking strategy took two forms: one was an increase in outreach to community volunteers; the other was "contracting out" some of the services they previously provided their clients internally.

Fortunately, volunteers responded and other hospital-based rape crisis services around the city picked up some of the slack. Because of this networking, Rape 10 remains open today. Networking is also viewed as a life and death issue for General 7. This organization is charged with developing networks among ethnic women, both domestically and globally. They work on a variety of substantive issues, but all relate to the specific needs of women with a particular ethnic heritage. Thus, making the connections among these women worldwide has taken on importance in and of itself. The executive director put it this way:

> If we don't have our network in place, we're out of business. I might as well take my shingle off the front door and go home. It doesn't matter what policy position we take or what funds we raise or what resources we develop. If the network isn't there to reach our women, we've failed. I've failed. (General 7, August 2, 1990)

Back to the Original Question

I started out this chapter by asking *why* women's nonprofits look the way they do. Which theory (or theories) offers the best explanation of organizational form? For bureaucracies and collectives, age provides the strongest explanation. The older the organization, the more bureaucratic it will be. The younger the organization, the more collective in structure it will be. This finding is consistent with the organizational life cycle literature. Ideology also helps to explain structure. Particularly, organizations with a feminist ideology (of a variety of kinds) are more likely to adopt bureaucratic structures over collectivist ones. This finding partially challenges the feminist literature on both theory and practice that claims an affinity between radical feminism and collectivism. Finally, organizational tasks help to explain organizational structure. Specifically, organizations with routine tasks are more likely to adopt bureaucratic structures than collectivist ones. This is a partial confirmation of the expectations generated from contingency theory.

For hybrid organizations, we have a different set of explanations. And, as discussed earlier, these explanations were generated from the data, as no theory explains why certain organizations adopt hybrid structures. We have found that size provides a lot of insight. Small organizations are far more likely to be pragmatic-collectives than professional in structure. Large organizations are more likely to be professional organizations than pragmatic-collectives. Organizational constituency is the second predictor of form. Organizations dominated by professionals (of a variety of kinds) are most likely to adopt the professional organizational form. Organizations that are dominated by minorities and/or serve minority populations primarily are most likely to adopt a pragmatic-collective form. Finally, organizations that are engaged in networking as the core of their work are most likely to be organized as pragmatic-collectives.

In the final chapter, I review the primary contributions of this research and consider the implications the findings have for both organizational theory and research on women's organizations.

5

CONCLUSION

I began this book with a number of expectations, only some of which were realized. I want to end by highlighting what I did *not* anticipate: the surprises and paradoxical findings.

First, given the theoretical preoccupation with the distinction between bureaucracy and collectives among organizational scholars and early women's movement organizers, I expected the empirical world to reflect this preoccupation. I thought I would find most women's nonprofits to be either bureaucratic or collective, with some hybrids (which combine the characteristics of the two). While I did find variation, I did not expect that the overwhelming majority of the action lies with the hybrids. Sixty-nine out of the ninety-five organizations (seventy-three percent) fall within the two hybrid categories.

Second, I thought there would be a particular association between feminist ideology and organizational form: Non-feminists and liberal feminists would adopt bureaucratic structures, and radical feminists would adopt collectivist structures. Instead, what I found was that organizations with a feminist ideology *of a variety of kinds* are more likely to be bureaucratic than collectivist. Moreover, the collectives in this population do not appear to be relatives of the progressive, leftist collectives that proliferated in this country during the 1960s. They are young and apolitical.

Third, I envisioned there would be some discussion about organizational structure among members of women's nonprofits, although certainly not to the extent to which early women's movement organizers were preoccupied with structure. In other words, I would *like* to say that professional organizations and pragmatic collectives are *conscious* creations of women in the nonprofit sphere; they are deliberate attempts to blend useful aspects of bureaucracy and useful elements of collectives. My preference, however, is contradicted by what the women say.

Clearly, there are examples of organizations whose members I interviewed that had (or continue to have) specific discussions about organizational structure (seven of the twenty-five organizations I interviewed). They researched other organizations' structures, experimented with different models, hired outsiders to advise them on organizational styles, and engaged in organizational "talk" about structure. There are other examples of organizations for which the issue of organizational structure is considered passé (four organizations): It is something they agonized over in the sixties, they have moved on to more important things, they are too busy saving women's lives to be worried about their organizational style. But overwhelmingly, the response I got from those I interviewed was a momentary silence and a nonresponse of sorts. The majority of women (fourteen of the twenty-five organizations) told me they have never talked about organizational structure, even in the early years. They claimed it "just emerged," it was "serendipitous," it happened without explicit discussion or a master plan. This is a distinct departure from women's organizations in the late 1960s and 1970s (Feit 1979; Freeman & MacDonald 1976-77; Schlesinger & Bart 1982; Sealander & Smith 1986; Seifer & Wertheimer 1979; Tanner 1970).

What implications do these unexpected findings have for organizational theory and research on women's organizations?

Implications for Organizational Theory

I have studied a class of organizations that has been too rarely the focus of empirical analyses by organizational sociologists: nonprofit groups *by* and *for* women. Adding women's nonprofits to organizational sociologists' databank on organizations, in and of itself, is an important contribution. We cannot answer the question whether women's organizations are unique or distinct from male-dominated organizations without first documenting women's organizational experiences in all their variation.

Second, in focusing on women's nonprofits from an organizational perspective, I am able to say something about the usefulness of conventional sociological theories of organizations for interpreting women's organizational experience. Are they helpful? Are they as general as they claim to be? Although I did not conduct a formal test of Rothschild-Whitt (1979), my analysis suggests that her conceptual framework (with modification) is applicable to the women's nonprofit sphere. Likewise, in varying ways, the organizational life cycle literature on age, contingency theory, and the scholarship on size helped me interpret why women's nonprofits look the way they do. But, despite the importance given to the organizational environment in the study of organizations in general, the environmental variables were of little significance in understanding why women's nonprofits adopt certain organizational forms.

Finally, and most important, my research suggests that theoretical attention needs to focus on hybrid organizations because that is where all the action is empirically. Yet the majority of theorizing about organizations has concentrated on the two extremes: bureaucracy and collectives. I have begun to add flesh to the notion of a "hybrid" organization by specifying the exact configuration of bureaucratic and collectivist elements that are blended in different ways in professional organizations and pragmatic collectives. A great deal of theorizing about hybrids, however, remains to be done. Organizational theorists would be wise to shift their efforts away from the two extreme types of organizations and concentrate instead on hybrid forms.

Implications for Research on Women's Organization

The mere existence of four distinct forms of organizations among women's nonprofits in New York City *and* the fact that the two hybrid forms are the most populated suggest that women have been willing to step outside both the bureaucratic mainstream and the collectivist alternative to innovate with hybrid forms. Pragmatic collectives dispense with some aspects of collectivism that have historically made this form of organization particularly time-consuming, impractical, and difficult for incorporating diversity in membership without compromising the essence of collectivism (shared decision-making and little division of labor). Professional organizations, while they have some elements of bureaucracy (most notably, a moderate amount of differentiation), are able to balance the emergent differences in status with collective decision making. The collective conscience that emerges among professional domains facilitates decision making by consensus and, at the same time, avoids the usual pitfalls of reaching consensus (for example, inefficiency). To prosper, research on women's organizations needs to focus on, and theorize about, hybrids *on their own terms* and not in the shadow of the bureaucratic/collectivist debate.

The findings here also suggest that women who are interested in forming organizations with an explicit feminist ideology are not constrained by organizational form. Most important, unlike what some feminist critics of bureaucracy have argued (Ferguson 1984), feminist principles and bureaucracy do not appear to be fundamentally incompatible. Women's nonprofits in New York City that adopt a feminist ideology are not only thriving with the formal bureaucratic form but are also innovating by combining aspects of both bureaucratic and collectivist structures.

In terms of the implications of the departure from organizational talk about structure that dominated women's groups in the sixties and early seventies, it is difficult to know, without additional information, whether this move is positive or negative. What does it mean to say an organization's structure "just emerged" without an explicit plan? Is it possible that only some members of an organization are privy to the conscious design?

The main findings of this study seem to beg the question: Is one organizational form more successful than another? The answer to this question, too, requires additional research. Staggenborg (1995) identifies three types of organizational successes for women's movement organizations. An organization is successful if it produces changes in policy and practices of formal institutions. Groups are successful if they contribute to cultural change. And, an organization is successful if it survives. The final type is considered successful because organizational survival means it created new resources for the ongoing representation and mobilization of the women's movement. Future research attempting to measure the relative success among these four organizational styles seems a likely, and important, next step.

APPENDIX

METHODOLOGY

Women's nonprofit organizations formed during the contemporary women's movement (1967-1988) in the five boroughs of New York City are the focus of this research. New York City was selected for its significance as a site for national and grassroots organizing by women and for its proximity to New Haven, Connecticut, where I resided at the time.

Identifying the Population

No comprehensive listing of women's nonprofits exists, so it was necessary to compile a list of organizations. My goal was to construct a list that was inclusive of all organizations that met a specific set of criteria. I used the following sources of information to complete this task: 1) twenty-one national and local directories of women's organizations, five of which have more than one edition (see "Directories Used To Compile List of Organizations" below); 2) profiles of national and local women's organizations maintained by the Women's Action Alliance in New York City; 3) lists of grantees funded by four New York City foundations specializing in the support of women's organizations; 4) a 1989 mailing list of a long-standing, grassroots feminist organization located in New York City; 5) local feminist periodicals, newspapers, and newsletters; and 6) social histories of the contemporary women's movement that made specific reference to New York City.

Organizations were selected from the sources above if they met the following criteria:

1. *Geographical location.* Organizations with mailing addresses in the five boroughs of New York City (Bronx, Brooklyn, Manhattan, Staten Island, and Queens) were included.

2. *Date of foundation.* Organizations founded between the years 1961 and 1989 were included. I selected 1961 as the starting point, as it is the earliest date identified in the literature in terms of the re-emergence of feminism in this country (see Freeman 1975:449). As it turned out, the organizations that participated in the study were founded between 1967 and 1988.

3. *Status of organization.* Only organizations that were in operation during the quantitative data collection phase of the project (October 31, 1989 to April 6, 1990) were included in the study. This decision introduces a bias toward "successful" and long-lived organizations.

4. *Type of organization.* I used the distinction between public goods- and private goods-oriented organizations to further specify the selection criteria: the former are included and the latter are not. Nonprofit service and political action organizations that produce services (or positive outcomes) that will not be consumed in their entirety, or even to a great extent by the groups' members (that is, public goods) are included. For-profit firms, professional interest groups, social clubs, and consciousness-raising groups that produce outcomes primarily consumed by the groups' members (that is, private goods) are excluded.

5. *Scope.* Local organizations, as well as national and international organizations with headquarters or branches in New York City were included. In the latter two cases, data were gathered only on the activities of the group in the local context. Coalitions or federations of organizations were excluded. However, whether a particular organization belongs to these larger networks became important information.

6. *Proximity to the bureaucratic order.* Both free-standing

organizations and those situated within the confines of a larger bureaucratic setting (for example, a rape crisis center in a hospital) qualified for inclusion. I adopted this approach in order to explore an interesting direction of inquiry on collectivist organizations. Musheno (1988:2) argues that the literature on alternative organizations is problematic because it assumes transformative organizations exist only external to complex bureaucracies. He presents a case for "defiant cells" operating within complex organizations that, through their alternative form, have the potential to "chip away at bureaucratic domination." Following his call for widening the boundaries of what constitutes a possible site for alternative organizations, I look for women's groups both within and outside bureaucracies. This is also consistent with Katzenstein's (1990) research that focuses on feminist organizations that exist within conventional institutions.

7. *Philosophy.* Originally, I set out to study feminist organizations. Since no comprehensive list of feminist groups in New York City exists, I relied on directories (and other sources listed above) of women's organizations to compile my initial list. The plan was then to use the first stage of data collection (the questionnaire) to weed out those women's organizations that do not self-identify as feminist. I anticipated that a small percentage would have to be excluded. I was wrong. As documented in Chapter 2, slightly less than half of the organizations do not consider their groups feminist ones (that is, they explicitly reject feminism, have never considered it, or are undecided). This finding was too interesting to side-step by eliminating them from the study (and I did not want to lose nearly half of my cases). So, what was originally a study of feminist organizations has become a study of women's organizations, some of which adopt a feminist philosophy.

This selection process resulted in a population of 239 women's nonprofit organizations.

Data Collection

Mail Survey. The initial phase of data collection consisted of a self-administered questionnaire directed at the entire population of New York City women's nonprofits. I adopted Dillman's (1978) "Total Design Method" (TDM) for mail surveys. This approach, which consists of a detailed recipe for mail survey construction, packaging, and implementation, has been developed to increase the likelihood of survey response. The questionnaire was designed to measure organizational form, the environment of each organization, and organizational tasks. The questionnaire was pretested by the directors (or spokeswomen) of five women's nonprofit organizations (four in Connecticut; one in Washington, D.C.) in October, 1989, and the survey was revised accordingly.

On October 31, 1989 the final version of the survey was mailed to the head of each of the 239 organizations identified above. The name of the director or spokeswoman of each organization was obtained through the most recent directory of organizations and was verified with a telephone call to each organization for which a phone number was available. In a number of cases I reached an answering machine; not all of these groups returned my call (even though I invited them to call me back collect).

A key aspect of TDM is a closely monitored system of follow-up mailings. Thus, I sent a follow-up postcard one week after the initial mailing (November 8, 1989), a follow-up letter and replacement survey approximately three weeks later (November 28, 1989), and a final follow-up letter and replacement survey approximately five weeks later (January 3, 1990). I adjusted Dillman's timing recommendation (two and six week follow-ups) slightly in order to work around the holidays. In addition, on December 7, 1989, December 15, 1989 and January 26, 1990 I made a series of phone calls to organizations that had not yet responded to my mailings, inquired as to their plans, and encouraged them to respond.

In the mailing and follow-up process, I obtained new information on 41 organizations that indicated they should be removed from the base population, leaving a new total of 198. Sixteen of these forty-one groups were no longer in operation. The remaining 25 did not meet all of the initial criteria (for example, I learned they were founded prior to the 1960s, they were for-profit, they moved outside New York City). Of the 198 organizations, 113 returned completed questionnaires, resulting in a response rate of fifty-seven percent. The "nonresponses" took three forms. In 64 cases, there was literally no response. For 14 organizations, the envelopes were returned by the post office marked "return to sender" (forwarding addressing unknown). In 7 cases, questionnaires were returned blank with a note indicating that the organization refused to participate.

Interviews and Field Notes. The second phase of data collection consisted of face-to-face interviews with organizational members of a sample of groups that returned completed surveys. The purpose of the interviews was to get more detailed information on a group of organizations, focusing particularly on the history of the organizations, how women talk about organizational structure, and changes in structure, work, and environment over time. I randomly selected 25 organizations and made arrangements to interview the head of each organization. In five instances, I interviewed two people. In a few cases, I met with someone other than the head of the organization. A total of 30 interviews were conducted between July 31, 1990 and March 26, 1992 (see "List of Interviewees" below).

Interviews lasted between 45 and 90 minutes. When possible, I tape-recorded the conversation and transcribed it in full afterwards. For interviews that were not tape-recorded I took notes during the session and filled in the detail immediately following the interview. The majority of the interviews took place at the respective organizational sites; in three cases, the interviews were conducted in private homes, as the organizations had no headquarters or physical space.

In addition, I took field notes of my trip to each interview and of the physical setting of the organization. I used public transportation (usually the subway) to get to the interview locations as I wanted to experience the organization as would a woman seeking their services (or traveling to work). To give you a sense of the New York City "community" of women's nonprofits, the trips ranged from a ten-minute subway ride from Grand Central Station to the Upper West Side to an hour and a half combination subway and cab ride from the same starting point to the southern end of Queens.

Organizational Documents. In the majority of cases where I carried out interviews, I also collected organizational documents that provided further information about the organization. The organizational documents I commonly gathered included brochures, newsletters, employee handbooks, organizational charts, newspaper clippings, and mission statements.

Directories Used to Compile List of Organizations

East Coast Asian Student Union. 1988. "Asian American Resource Directory," pp. 30-35 in *Asian American Spirit.* Boston: ECASU/New England.

Encyclopedia of Associations, 1961-1988. Detroit, MI: Gale Research Company.

Federation of Organizations for Professional Women. 1984/1986. *A Women's Yellow Book.* Washington, D.C.:FOPW.

Felmley, Jenrose, ed. 1986. *Directory of National Women's Organizations.* Allstate Insurance Companies and Sears, Roebuck, and Company.

First National Women's Network Directory. 1980. NY: Working Woman.

Gager, Nancy, ed. 1974. *Women's Rights Almanac.* New York: Harper and Row.

Gardner, Richard. 1976/1984. *Alternative America.* Cambridge, MA: Gardner.

Harrison, Cynthia Ellen. 1975. *Women's Movement Media: A Source Guide.* New York: R.R. Bowker.

Index/Directory of Women's Media. 1987. Washington, D.C.: Women's Institute for Freedom of the Press.

Kruzas, Anthony T. 1982. *Social Service Organizations and Agencies Directory.* Detroit, MI: Gale Research Co.

Library and Information Sources on Women: A Guide to Collections in the Greater New York Area. 1988. New York: The Feminist Press at the City University of New York.

Merrill Doss, Martha, ed. 1986. *Women's Organizations: A National Directory.* Garrett Park, MD: Garrett Park Press.

Paulsen, Kathryn and Ryan A. Kuhn. 1976. *Woman's Almanac.* New York: J.B. Lippincott.

Rogerson, Anita, ed. n.d. *Women's Resource Guide to NYC.* New York: NOW-New York City.

Snyder, Peggy, ed. 1986. *New York Women: A County-by-County Directory of Organizations and Services.* New York: New York State Division for Women.

Steinman, Wayne. 1989. *Lesbian and Gay Services/Resources Directory, New York Metropolitan Area.* New York: The City of New York Office of the Comptroller.

Williamson, Jane, Diane Winston, and Wanda Wooten, eds. 1980. *Women's Action Almanac.* New York: William and Morrow Co.

Women's Action Alliance. 1981. *Women Helping Women: A State-by-State Directory of Services.* New York: Neal-Schuman.

Women's Organizations: A New York City Directory. 1982/1986-87/1989-90. New York: New York City Commission on Women.

Women's Organizations and Leaders Directory. 1973/1986. Washington, D.C.: Today/Triangle Press.

Working Woman Project: A WCBS-TV Guide to Resources for the Working Woman, n.d. NY: WCBS-TV.

List of Interviewees

Community Center 3, co-coordinator, August 20, 1990
Counseling 4, executive director, December 5, 1991
Domestic Violence 4, program coordinator,
    March 13, 1992
Domestic Violence 7, executive director, August 1, 1990
Education 1, executive director, August 1, 1990
Education 3, co-director, March 5, 1992
Education 3, co-director, March 5, 1992
Employment 3, executive director, November 7, 1991
Employment 5, director, October 31, 1991
Employment 7, director of education, July 31, 1990
Employment 7, director of research and development,
    July 31, 1990
Employment 9, director, December 2, 1991
General 7, director, August 2, 1990
General 10, president, March 13, 1992
General 10, executive director, March 26, 1992
General 13, board member, March 26, 1992
General 17, executive director, October 23, 1990
Health Education 2, associate director of management and public
    education, October 25, 1991
Health Education 4, executive director, October 31, 1991
Health Education 9, program coordinator, August 20, 1990
Law 4, director of planning and development, December 5, 1991
Rape 1, founding member, October 9, 1991
Rape 1, member, October 18, 1991
Rape 2, program coordinator, March 4, 1992
Rape 6, coordinator, August 6, 1990
Rape 6, long-time volunteer, October 5, 1990
Rape 7, assistant director, November 11, 1991
Rape 9, director, December 5, 1991
Rape 10, coordinator, October 9, 1991
University Center 6, director, October 9, 1990

Data Analysis

Factor Analysis (Chapter 2)

I began with Rothschild-Whitt's (1979) eight dimensions of organizational structure, operationalizing each one as follows. I ended up with a total of forty-six measures.

1. *Authority* measures who makes decisions in three different hypothetical scenarios. The responses range from the members of the organization as a group, to a subgroup of the organization, to an individual. The first scenario is a decision about a staff member's request for a six-month leave (AUTHOR3).[1] The second scenario is a decision about how to discipline a staff member who has made $300 worth of unauthorized long distance phone calls (AUTHOR4). The third scenario involves making a decision about hiring an executive director (or equivalent) (AUTHOR5).

2. *Differentiation* is measured in terms of the number of distinct job titles there are in the organization (DIFF2) and the percentage of these jobs that are permanent positions (DIFF3).

3. *Rules* are measured according to how many different kinds of written rules an organization maintains, ranging from zero to five (the five are job descriptions, contracts of employment, personnel procedure manual, written policies, and organizational by-laws) (RULE). Second, the specificity of these rules is measured on a scale from one to six (RUL6). Third, the use of formal, written rules and regulations in actual decision making is measured in the decision-making scenario about a staff member's request for a leave. RULA2 measures the importance (on a scale from one to seven) of written policies and procedures, RULA3 measures the importance of individual judgment, RULA4 measures the importance of the fairness of the request, and RULA5 measures the importance of the opinions of the other members of the group.

4. *Social control* is assessed by the number of formal control mechanisms that are present in the organization, ranging from zero to four (the four are performance evaluations, disciplinary procedures, written rules for handling misconduct, and employee grievance

procedures) (CONTROL). Methods of informal control are measured in terms of the homogeneity of membership, homogeneity in both demographics and political orientation. Using a scale, respondents are asked to measure the homogeneity/heterogeneity of the membership according to gender (DEM1), race (DEM2), income (DEM3), education (DEM4), political beliefs (SR1), and views of feminism/women's issues (SR3).

The use of formal versus informal means of control in actual decision making are captured in a decision-making scenario on what to do with a staff member who made unauthorized phone calls. SCA1 measures the importance (on a scale from one to five) of disciplinary procedures. SCA2 measures the importance of individual judgment. SCA3 measures the importance of sanctions outlined in written policies. And SCA4 measures the importance of personal appeals by other members to pay back the money.

5. *Social relations* vary by degree of impersonality among organizational members. The first two measures concern the extent to which organizational members spend time together outside the organization, worded in two different ways (SR4, SR6). The second two measures capture the degree to which members consider each other friends, again with a change in wording (SR2, SR5). All four are measured on a scale from one to seven, ranging from strongly agree to strongly disagree.

6. *Recruitment* refers to the kind of criteria used in selecting individuals for organizational membership. Criteria range from being political or subjective to objective. Political or subjective criteria include the applicant's personality or character (REC2), the endorsement by a member of the organization (REC4), the recommendation of someone outside the organization (REC5), and the applicant's political views (REC7). Objective criteria include the applicant's experience (REC1), the applicant's specialized training (REC3), and the applicant's education (REC6).

7. *Incentives* have to do with the types of organizational inducements or rewards that are meaningful to organizational participants, ranging from normative to material. Normative incentives consist of challenging or interesting work (INC2), friendships with coworkers

(INC3), shared purpose among coworkers (INC5), opportunity to effect social change (INC7), personal empowerment (INC9), recognition in the community (INC11), and chances to use skills (INC12). Material incentives are wages or salaries (INC1), opportunities for promotion (INC4), vacation or time-off (INC6), health insurance (INC8), and child care services (INC10).

8. *Social stratification* involves the extent to which monetary rewards are distributed equally or unequally among organizational members. PAYDIFF is measured by calculating the difference between the highest earner's salary and the lowest earner's salary in the organization.

I used exploratory factor analysis, particularly principal component factor analysis, to assess the underlying patterns or relationships that exist for the forty-six variables that measure organizational structure. Using the SAS FACTOR procedure, I selected the orthogonal method of extraction. With the orthogonal method, the factors are extracted so that the factor axes are kept at ninety degrees. In other words, each factor is assumed to be independent (Hair et al. 1984). To facilitate interpretation, I employed the VARIMAX rotation option. The goal of VARIMAX is to simplify the columns of the factor matrix (SAS 1985).

I used both the scree test and latent root criteria for determining the optimum number of factors to extract. The scree test plots the eigenvalues against the number of factors in their order of extraction. I then looked at the shape of the resulting curve to determine the cut-off point. A rule of thumb is to identify the point at which the curve begins to straighten out. I compared the results of this with the results of the latent root criterion, which selects only the factors that have eigenvalues greater than one. After considering several different trial rotations, I selected seven factors. This final factor solution was then analyzed and I assigned meaning to the pattern of factor loadings (as described in Chapter 2) (Hair et al. 1984; Jackson and Borgatta 1981). Computer output of each stage of the analysis is available from the author.

The analysis resulted in the seven factors presented in Table A.1. I have named factor 1 "Material Incentives and Formal Structures." The variables with high loadings on this factor include material

TABLE A.1
Rotated Factor Pattern

	Material incentives and formal structures	Normative incentives	Decision-making authority	Formal decision-making criteria	Shared beliefs and time	Informal decision-making criteria	Differentiation
	Factor 1	Factor 2	Factor 3	Factor 4	Factor 5	Factor 6	Factor 7
INC6	.90361						
INC1	.90036						
INC8	.89665						
DIFF3	.77260						
INC4	.75543						
RULE	.60645						
CONTROL	.57487						
INC2		.78723					
INC7		.78404					
INC5		.76955					
INC12		.67085					
INC9		.60258					
INC3		.52018					
AUTHOR4			.79546				
AUTHOR5			.76294				
AUTHOR3			.72159				
PAYDIFF			.56344				
SCA3				.82664			
SCA1				.76110			
RULA2				.64914			
SR1					.71598		
SR6					.70566		
SR3					.63113		
REC7					.58325		
SR4					.55978		
RULA4						.87933	
RULA5						.74822	
RULA3						-.72285	
DEM3							.66246
DEM4							.63339
DIFF2							.52080

Variance explained by each factor

	Factor 1	Factor 2	Factor 3	Factor 4	Factor 5	Factor 6	Factor 7
	5.393026	3.071304	2.843996	2.484561	2.428367	2.197655	1.751639

N=95

incentives (INC6, INC1, INC8, INC4), permanency in job positions (DIFF3), formal rules (RULE) and formal social controls (CONTROL). Factor 2 represents "Normative Incentives" and includes six measures of normative incentives (INC2, INC7, INC5, INC12, INC9 INC3). Factor 3 portrays "Decision-making Authority" and includes all three original authority measures (AUTHOR4, AUTHOR5, AUTHOR3) and the only measure for social stratification (PAYDIFF). Factor 4 stands for "Formal Decision-making Criteria" and includes the use of written sanctions (SCA3), use of disciplinary procedures (SCA1), and use of written policy (RULA2). Factor 5 represents "Shared Beliefs and Time" and combines three measures of shared political beliefs (SR1, SR3, REC7) and two variables that measure the extent to which members spend time together outside work (SR6, SR4). Factor 6 is labeled "Informal Decision-making Criteria" and consists of three measures of informal decision making (RULA4, RULA5, RULA3). "Differentiation" best captures factor 7, which contains the measure for the number of job titles (DIFF2) and measures of economic (DEM3) and educational diversity (DEM4) among organizational members.

Cluster Analysis (Chapter 3)

I used cluster analysis to categorize the organizations into a small number of meaningful and mutually exclusive subgroups. The goal of this analytic technique is to identify homogeneous subgroups, so we are looking for similarities among the groups along the previously identified seven structural dimensions. My use of cluster analysis is exploratory; I am not concerned here with hypothesis testing.

Using the FASTCLUS procedure in SAS, the observations were divided into clusters based on Euclidean distances. Thus, observations that are close to each other are assigned to the same cluster; those that are far apart are assigned to different clusters (SAS 1985). I did various trial runs specifying two through ten clusters. To decide how many clusters to use in the final analysis, I plotted the Pseudo F statistic for each number of clusters (ten, nine, eight, etc.) and the expected R-square for each number of clusters. These graphs indicated that the optimal number of clusters was three or four. To decide between the two, I generated means for each factor (or dimension) by cluster and plotted these scores. The four cluster solution was easiest to interpret and made the best substantive sense (Aldenderfer and Blashfield 1985; Guerlain 1989). Computer output of each stage of the analysis is available from the author.

Table A.2 reports the cluster means and standard deviations for each of the organizational dimensions. A cluster mean is calculated by averaging the factor scores of all cases in a particular cluster on one particular dimension (e.g., decision-making authority). While its absolute value has meaning, here we will be more concerned with its value relative to the other means for a particular dimension across clusters. Therefore, under each mean, I indicate its level: high (H), medium (M) or low (L).

Because the overall mean for each of the dimensions is not the same (for example, overall mean for decision-making authority is .075, mean for differentiation is .669), my criteria for determining whether a value is high, medium or low is based on the value's relationship to the overall mean for that particular dimension. High indicates a value greater than .5 above the overall mean for the dimension. Medium represents a value that is -.5 to .5 around the overall mean for the dimension. Low stands for a value that is less than -.5 below the overall mean for the dimension. Table A.3 lists the overall means for each of the seven dimensions. Prior to establishing these cutoffs, I generated bar graphs of the clusters on each factor score to verify that each is distributed normally about their mean.

TABLE A.2
**Cluster Means and Standard Deviations for
Dimensions of Organizational Structure**

Organizational Dimension	Cluster			
	1 Bureaucratic	2 Professional	3 Pragmatic Collective	4 Collective
Material Incentive	.506	-.370	-.019	.166
and Formal Structure	(.63)	(1.12)	(1.01)	(.81)
	M	L	M	M
Normative Incentive	-.155	-.355	-.163	2.382
	(.64)	(.50)	(.66)	(1.32)
	L	L	L	H
Decision-Making	.677	-.430	.011	-.183
Authority	(.83)	(.95)	(.97)	(.99)
	H	L	M	M
Formal Decision-	-.125	.477	-.230	-.031
Making Criteria	(.91)	(.94)	(1.06)	(.60)
	M	M	M	M
Shared Beliefs and Time	-.571	.515	-.229	.845
	(.69)	(.86)	(.99)	(.91)
	L	M	L	M
Informal Decision-	.114	.330	-.276	.152
Making Criteria	(1.10)	(.96)	(.93)	(1.01)
	M	M	L	M
Differentiation	1.048	.503	-.711	-.171
	(.75)	(.56)	(.73)	(.94)
	H	M	L	L

N=95
Number in parenthesis = standard deviation
L=LOW (less than -.5 below the mean)
M=MEDIUM (-.5 to .5 around the mean)
H=HIGH (more than .5 above the mean)

TABLE A.3
Overall Means for Each Structural Dimension

Organizational Dimension	Overall Mean
Material Incentives and Formal Structures	.283
Normative Incentives	1.709
Decision-Making Authority	.075
Formal Decision-Making Authority	.091
Shared Beliefs and Time	.560
Informal Decision-Making Criteria	.320
Differentiation	.669

N=95

NOTES

Chapter One

1. I use the terms organizational *form*, organizational *structure*, and organizational *style* interchangeably to refer to the overall structural characterization of an organization.

Chapter Two

1. The survey question read, "Does your group consider itself a *feminist* organization either in membership or purpose?" The response options were: 1) this subject has not come up; 2) this subject has come up, but is unresolved; 3) no; and 4) yes. The executive director (or equivalent) of each organization completed the survey. This measure is appropriate in that I was interested in determining the official stance of the organization as a whole. It is important to note, however, that individual members may consider themselves feminists or members other than the executive director may have different interpretations of the organization's official position regarding feminism.

2. Joyce Rothschild-Whitt's work was originally published in the *American Sociological Review* in 1979. Later, Joyce Rothschild and J. Allen Whitt came out with a book (1986), a chapter of which is the earlier article in its original form.

3. For a discussion of how each dimension was operationalized and the details of the factor analyses, see the Appendix.

4. As you can see by comparing this table with Table 2.7, there is a substantial amount of overlap between the factors generated here and the original dimensions proposed by Rothschild-Whitt.

5. There are exceptions to this claim that I will return to in Chapter 3.

Chapter Three

1. Due to missing information, the total number is reduced from 113 to ninety-five organizations. All the remaining analyses are based on these ninety-five cases.

2. The three decision-making scenarios are as follows:

> Scenario 1: The assistant director (or equivalent) of your organization requests a six-month leave of absence from her job for personal reasons.

> Scenario 2: You have been informed that the assistant director (or equivalent) of your organization has made unauthorized, personal long distance phone calls amounting to $300.

> Scenario 3: You have recently handed in your resignation. You have agreed to stay on and help in the process of finding your replacement.

The respondents were asked how important a number of factors were in making each decision and who was responsible for making the decision.

3. I want to respond to those of you who are thinking that this discussion sounds more like Talcott Parsons' romanticization of the medical profession than a description of doctors in the real world. All I can say is this: I am not describing the medical profession as a whole, but a setting where medical professionals (and others) come together. Perhaps because the medical profession itself is hierarchical, impersonal, and authoritarian, there is no need to replicate these formal structures in a particular setting. Therefore, when we go to measure such characteristics in an organization dominated by professionals, they are nowhere to be found. That does not mean that they do not get played out in the organization; it means that their origin is external to the organization.

Appendix

1. In the following discussion, I include each variable name in upper case letters in parentheses. These are for identification purposes only; the names and numbers included in these labels will not necessarily make substantive sense to the reader. For example, there are three measures of authority (AUTHOR3, AUTHOR4, AUTHOR5). There is no AUTHOR1 and AUTHOR2.

REFERENCES

Aldenderfer, Mark S. and Roger K. Blashfield. 1985. *Cluster Analysis*. Beverly Hills: Sage.

Barnett, Bernice McNair. 1995. "Black Women's Collectivist Movement Organizations: Their Struggles during the 'Doldrums'." Pp. 199-219 in *Feminist Organizations: Harvest of the New Women's Movement*, edited by Myra Marx Ferree and Patricia Yancey Martin. Philadelphia: Temple.

Bendix, Reinhard. 1968. "Bureaucracy." Pp. 206-219 in *International Encyclopedia of the Social Sciences*, Volume 2, edited by David L. Sills. New York: MacMillan and Free Press.

Blau, Peter M. 1970. "A Formal Theory of Differentiation in Organizations." *American Sociological Review* 35(2):201-218.

Brown, Helen. 1992. *Women Organising*. NY: Routledge.

Browne, Karen. 1976. "Reassessing Basics." *Quest: A Feminist Quarterly* 2(3):31-37.

Burns, Tom. 1971. "Mechanistic and Organismic Structures." Pp. 43-55 in *Organization Theory*, edited by D.S. Pugh. England: Penguin Books.

Carden, Maren Lockwood. 1974. *The New Feminist Movement*. New York: Russell Sage.

Dillman, Don A. 1978. *Mail and Telephone Surveys: The Total Design Method.* New York: John Wiley.

DiMaggio, Paul J. and Walter W. Powell. 1983. "The Iron Cage Revisited: Institutional Isomorphism and Collective Rationality in Organizational Fields." *American Sociological Review* 48:147-160.

Echols, Alice. 1989. *Daring to be Bad: Radical Feminism in America 1967-1975.* Minneapolis: University of Minnesota Press.

Evans, Sara. 1979. *Personal Politics: The Roots of Women's Liberation in the Civil Rights Movement and the New Left.* New York: Vintage.

Feit, Rona F. 1979. "Organizing for Political Power: The National Women's Political Caucus." Pp. 184-208 in *Women Organizing: An Anthology,* edited by Bernice Cummings and Victoria Schuck. Metuchen, NJ: Scarecrow.

Ferguson, Kathy E. 1984. *The Feminist Case Against Bureaucracy.* Philadelphia: Temple University Press.

Ferree, Myra Marx and Beth B. Hess. 1994. *Controversy and Coalition: The New Feminist Movement Across Three Decades of Change.* New York: Twayne.

Freeman, Alexa and Nancy MacDonald. 1976-77. "The Feminist Workplace." *Quest: A Feminist Quarterly* 3(3):65-73.

Freeman, Jo. 1974. "The Tyranny of Structurelessness." Pp. 202-214 in *Women in Politics,* edited by Jane S. Jacquette. New York: John Wiley and Sons.

Freeman, Jo. 1975. *The Politics of Women's Liberation.* New York: David McKay.

Giddens, Anthony. 1982. *Profiles and Critiques in Social Theory.* Berkeley: University of California Press.

Gottfried, Heidi and Penny Weiss. 1994. "A Compound Feminist Organization: Purdue University's Council on the Status of Women." *Women & Politics* 14(2):23-44.

Guerlain, Natalie M. 1989. "Reliability, Discrimination, and Common Sense in Cluster Analysis." Pp. 325-334 in *Sawtooth Software Conference Proceedings*. Ketchum, Idaho: Sawtooth Software.

Hair, Joseph F., Rolph E. Anderson, Ronald L. Tatham, Bernie J. Grablowsky. 1984. *Multivariate Data Analysis*. New York: Macmillan.

Hall, Richard H. 1963. "The Concept of Bureaucracy: An Empirical Assessment." *American Journal of Sociology* 69:32-40.

Hall, Richard H. 1968. "Professionalization and Bureaucratization." *American Sociological Review* 33:92-104.

Iannello, Kathleen P. 1992. *Decisions Without Hierarchy: Feminist Interventions in Organization Theory and Practice*. New York: Routledge.

Jackson, David J. and Edgar F. Borgatta. 1981. *Factor Analysis and Measurement in Sociological Research*. Beverly Hills: Sage.

Johnson, John M. 1981. "Program Enterprise and Official Cooptation in the Battered Women's Shelter Movement." *American Behavioral Scientist* 24(6):827-842.

Katzenstein, Mary Fainsod. 1990. "Feminism within American Institutions: Unobtrusive Mobilization in the 1980s." *Signs* 16(1):27-54.

Kimberly, John R. 1976. "Organizational Size and the Structuralist Perspective: A Review, Critique and Proposal." *Administrative Science Quarterly* 21(4):571-597.

Kornegger, Peggy. 1975. "Anarchism: The Feminist Connection." *The Second Wave* 4:26-37.

Leidner, Robin. 1991. "Stretching the Boundaries of Liberalism: Democratic Innovation in a Feminist Organization." *Signs* 16(2):263-289.

Litwak, Eugene. 1961. "Models of Bureaucracy which Permit Conflict." *American Journal of Sociology* 67:177-184.

Mansbridge, Jane. 1984. "Feminism and the Forms of Freedom." Pp. 472-481 in *Critical Studies in Organization and Bureaucracy*, edited by Frank Fischer and Carmen Sirianni. Philadelphia: Temple.

Martin, Gloria. 1986. *Socialist Feminism: The First Decade 1966-1976*. Seattle, WA: Freedom Socialist Publications.

Martin, Patricia Yancey. 1990. "Rethinking Feminist Organizations." *Gender & Society* 4(2):182-206.

Matthews, Nancy A. 1994. *Confronting Rape: The Feminist Anti-Rape Movement and the State*. New York: Routledge.

Michels, Robert. 1962. *Political Parties: A Sociological Study of the Oligarchical Tendencies of Modern Democracy*. New York: Free Press.

Milofsky, Carl. 1981. "Structure and Process in Community Self-Help Organizations." New Haven: Yale Program on Non-Profit Organizations, Working Paper No. 17.

Musheno, Michael C. 1988. "Internal Defiance of Bureaucratic Domination: Searching for Other Collectives." Discussion Essay for Roundtable on Pluralizing Inquiry of Collectivist Organizations and Bureaucratic Domination, Annual Meeting of the Law & Society Association, Vail, CO, June 9-12.

O'Sullivan, Liz. 1976. "Organizing for Impact." *Quest 2*(3):68-80.

Perkins, Dennis N.T., Veronica F. Nieva, and Edward Lawler III. 1983. *Managing Creation: The Challenge of Building a New Organization*. New York: John Wiley.

Perrow, Charles. 1967. "A Framework for Comparative Organizational Analysis." *American Sociological Review* 32(2):194-208.

Perrow, Charles. 1986. *Complex Organizations: A Critical Essay*, third edition. New York: Random House.

Powell, Walter W. 1987. "Hybrid Organizational Arrangements: New Form or Transitional Development?" *California Management Review* 30(1):67-87.

Pugh, Derek S., David J. Hickson, C. R. Hinings, and C. Turner. 1968. "Dimensions of Organization Structure." *Administrative Science Quarterly* 13:65-105.

Radical Women. 1973. *Manifesto: Theory, Program, and Structure*. Seattle, WA: Radical Women Publications.

Reinelt, Claire. 1994. "Fostering Empowerment, Building Community: The Challenge for State-Funded Feminist Organizations." *Human Relations* 47(6):685-705.

Reinelt, Claire. 1995. "Moving onto the Terrain of the State: The Battered Women's Movement and the Politics of Engagement," Pp. 84-104 in *Feminist Organizations: Harvest of the New Women's Movement*, edited by Myra Marx Ferree and Patricia Yancey Martin. Philadelphia: Temple University Press.

Rhinestein, Max. 1954. *Max Weber on Law in Economy and Society*. New York: Simon and Schuster.

Rodriguez, Noelie Maria. 1988. "Transcending Bureaucracy: Feminist Politics at a Shelter for Battered Women." *Gender & Society* 2(2):214-227.

Rothschild, Joan. 1976. "Taking Our Future Seriously." *Quest* 2(3):17-30.

Rothschild, Joyce and J. Allen Whitt. 1986. *The Cooperative Workplace: Potentials and Dilemmas of Organizational Democracy and Participation.* New York: Cambridge University Press.

Rothschild-Whitt, Joyce. 1979. "The Collectivist Organization: An Alternative to Rational-Bureaucratic Models." *American Sociological Review* 44:509-527.

Russell, Raymond. 1985. "Employee Ownership and Internal Governance." *Journal of Economic Behavior and Organization* 6:217-241.

Ryan, Barbara. 1992. *Feminism and the Women's Movement: Dynamics of Change in Social Movement Ideology and Activism.* NY: Routledge.

SAS Institute Inc. 1985. *SAS User's Guide: Statistics,* version 5 edition. Cary, NC: SAS Institute.

Schlesinger, Melinda Bart and Pauline B. Bart. 1982. "Collective Work and Self-Identity: Working in a Feminist Illegal Abortion Collective," Pp. 139-153 in *Workplace Democracy and Social Change*, edited by Frank Lindenfeld and Joyce Rothschild-Whitt. Boston: Porter Sargent.

Sealander, Judith and Dorothy Smith. 1986. "The Rise and Fall of Feminist Organizations in the 1970s: Dayton As a Case Study." *Feminist Studies* 12(2):321-341.

Seifer, Nancy and Barbara Wertheimer. 1979. "New Approaches to Collective Power: Four Working Women's Organizations," Pp. 152-183 in *Women Organizing: An Anthology*, edited by Bernice Cummings and Victoria Schuck. Metuchen, NJ: Scarecrow.

Staggenborg, Suzanne. 1989. "Stability and Innovation in the Women's Movement: A Comparison of Two Movement Organizations." *Social Problems* 36(1):75-92.

Staggenborg, Suzanne. 1995. "Can Feminist Movements be Successful?" Pp. 334-355 in *Feminist Organizations: Harvest of the New Women's Movement*, edited by Myra Marx Ferree and Patricia Yancey Martin. Philadelphia: Temple.

Stinchcombe, Arthur L. 1965. "Social Structure and Organizations," Pp. 142-191 in *Handbook of Organizations*, edited by James G. March. Chicago: Rand McNally.

Sullivan, Gail. 1982. "Cooptation of Alternative Services: The Battered Women's Movement as a Case Study." *Catalyst* 14(2):39-56.

Swidler, Ann. 1979. *Organization Without Authority: Dilemmas of Social Control in Free Schools*. Cambridge: Harvard University Press.

Tanner, Leslie B. (ed.) 1970. *Voices from Women's Liberation*. New York: New American Library.

Udy, Stanley H. 1959. "'Bureaucracy' and 'Rationality' in Weber's Organization Theory: An Empirical Study." *American Sociological Review* 24:791-795.

Ware, Cellestine. 1970. *Woman Power: The Movement for Women's Liberation*. NY: Tower.

Weber, Max. 1978. *Economy and Society*, Volumes 1 and 2, edited by Guenther Roth and Claus Wittich. Berkeley: University of California Press.

Woodul, Jennifer. 1984. "What's This About Feminist Businesses?" Pp.247-250 in *Feminist Frameworks: Alternative Theoretical Accounts of the Relations Between Women and Men*, edited by Alison M. Jaggar and Paula S. Rothenberg. New York: McGraw-Hill.

Zucker, Lynne G. 1983. "Organizations as Institutions." *Research in the Sociology of Organizations* 2:1-47.

INDEX

ABOUT THE AUTHOR

Rebecca L. Bordt is Assistant Professor of Sociology at the University of Notre Dame. She received an M.S. in Justice Studies from Arizona State University in 1985 and a Ph.D. in Sociology from Yale University in 1994.

Her research and teaching interests include the sociology of organizations, gender studies, and criminology. She has published on feminist collectives, gender differences in criminal court sentencing, and informal dispute resolution.

Her academic interests are enriched by her experience in various nonprofit organizations. She was a board member of Inside-Out: Citizens United for Prison Reform, Inc., in Connecticut from 1986-1992, a founding member of the Graduate Feminist Women in the Social Sciences at Yale University from 1986-1987, and is currently on the board of directors of Dismas of Michiana, a reconciliation-based transitional community of ex-offenders and college students in South Bend, Indiana.